The Martyrdom of Collins Catch the Bear

The Martyrdom of
Collins
Catch the Bear

GERRY SPENCE

Seven Stories Press
New York • Oakland • Liverpool

A SEVEN STORIES PRESS FIRST EDITION

Seven Stories Press
140 Watts Street
New York, NY 10013
www.sevenstories.com

College professors and high school and middle school teachers may
order free examination copies of Seven Stories Press titles.
To order, visit www.sevenstories.com
or send a fax on school letterhead to (212) 226-1411.

Library of Congress Cataloging-in-Publication Data

Names: Spence, Gerry, author.
Title: The martyrdom of Collins Catch the Bear / Gerry Spence.
Description: A Seven Stories Press first edition. | New York : Seven
Stories Press, [2019] | Includes bibliographical references. |
Identifiers: LCCN 2019056551 (print) | LCCN 2019056552 (ebook) | ISBN
9781609809669 (trade paperback) | ISBN 9781609809676 (ebook)
Subjects: LCSH: Collins Catch the Bear--Trials, litigation, etc. | Lakota
Indians--Legal status, laws, etc.--South Dakota--History--20th century.
| Indians, Treatment of--North America--History--20th century. | Indians
of North America--Government relations--1934- | Trials (Murder)--South
Dakota--History--20th century. | Discrimination in criminal justice
administration--South Dakota--History--20th century.
Classification: LCC E99.T34 S64 2019 (print) | LCC E99.T34 (ebook) | DDC
978.004/9752440092 [B]--dc23
LC record available at https://lccn.loc.gov/2019056551
LC ebook record available at https://lccn.loc.gov/2019056552

Book design by Jon Gilbert

Printed in the USA

9 8 7 6 5 4 3 2 1

I dedicate this book to Jim Leach, a lawyer who truly represents devotion. Jim counseled and fought for Collins Catch the Bear both in and out of court for most of Collins's adult life. He did so without pay or reward of fame and in the face of hopeless legal and personal obstacles. He never gave up. In his dedication to his client, he is a role model for all of us.

Prologue

Time has a way of amusing itself. But it soon grows bored with our heroic struggles, flips them into a pile of mortal foolishness, and forgets them. I thought this story was about an Indian who was assaulted by Time's cruel, blinding decoy of hope, an Indian who fought back. History decrees our heroes. But history is often as foolish and as fickle as we.

I'd written something like a hundred pages on an old electric typewriter—my writer's weapon in those days—about my defense of Collins Catch the Bear, a Lakota Sioux who'd been charged with the murder of a white man. Then Catch the Bear, without offering reason or explanation, which was his way, ordered that I stop writing. So, I tossed my work onto the top shelf of a closet, and the pages yellowed and curled in protest for nearly thirty years.

In the decades that hurtled by, I lost contact with Catch the Bear. I remembered him as a bright, articulate young man who'd become dedicated to the cause of Indian rights, trying his lawyers' patience with a host of problems, which I recount in the pages that follow. Then: silence. I supposed he was either in prison or rotting away on the reservation in South Dakota. Then, a short time ago, fate intervened, and I found myself freed to tell his story.

America's attention to Indian rights, as capricious as it has been, was recently revived when representatives of 280 tribes from across the nation joined to peaceably protest the Dakota Access Pipeline's invasion of sacred Indian lands in North Dakota. Indian demonstrations, both peaceful and deadly, were nothing new in the Dakotas. In 1973 the American Indian Movement (AIM), championed by Russell Means, the infamous Indian renegade, occupied the Indian village of Wounded Knee, in South Dakota, in a hostile seventy-one-day siege in which two Indians lost their lives and a federal officer was shot and paralyzed.

In 1982, the Lakota Sioux established the Yellow Thunder

Camp, just outside Rapid City, South Dakota. This unauthorized encroachment on the National Forest was the progeny of the same Russell Means of the 1973 Wounded Knee occupation. Both whites and Indians had their say regarding the camp, and the killing continued: on July 21, Clarence Tollefson, a forty-nine-year-old white man from Rapid City was fatally shot at the camp. Such deadly confrontations seemed sealed in the genes of history.

According to the verbiage of Rodney Lefholz, then the state's prosecutor, who'd recently announced his candidacy for South Dakota attorney general, it was one Collins Catch the Bear who had shot and killed Tollefson, and justice demanded that he be forthwith charged, tried, convicted, and thereafter permanently eliminated from the population. In those days (and perhaps today in some quarters of the state), Indians were viewed with approximately the same affection as coyotes, rats, and other vermin.

An elder of the Sacred Stone Camp appearing in support of the Standing Rock

I'd been coaxed into the case by Jim Leach, of Rapid City, a kid who'd been out of law school a few years but not long enough to shed his romantic notions, like Don Quixote in his chivalric search for justice. Leach was irrevocably wedded to the case. Why, I didn't know. But one thing I'd learned (the hard way) was that embracing virtue often leads to unforeseen misadventures. Catch the Bear's trial was imminent, and Leach said he needed my help defending him.

Before I take on any case, I try to discover who the client is. I want to know something about the seed and roots as well as the blossom. Collins Catch the Bear offered no remarkable history except multiple convictions for various crimes, and when I asked him about his life, he was often unresponsive or his answers vague. Moreover, he was unable to pay the first penny for his defense, covering not even the barest of expenses.

I've long contended that lawyers ought not commit to a case unless they've been able to discover, after a charitable search,

Collins Catch the Bear, March 1993

something in the client they can care about at the heart level. I've represented alleged killers and thieves and crooks of many stripes, and I've found that if one cuts through the hard, often hostile survival armor of even the most depraved, one will often find a tortured soul: a child wounded by parents hopelessly lost to drugs and alcohol or, too often, stifled by utter poverty—but under it all, a human being worth caring about.

For Catch the Bear's part, he often came off like a cipher in glasses. Perhaps, I thought, the tribal records would furnish more insights than the man seemed capable of providing. So, it was there that Leach and I started our archeological dig in search of Collins Catch the Bear. And, indeed, what we found was a young, lost Sioux in search of the same elusive person: himself.

To bring me up to speed on the case, Jim Leach provided me with boxes of forgotten records, some incomplete, the events they related inviting careful reconstruction. Some lapses in the records were filled by the recollections of people who were there and by suppositions based on our own best judgment. In my research, I tried to stay in tune with the requiem that seemed to accompany Catch the Bear's life. As a lawyer, I was, from time to time, required to create characters and conversations to illustrate the carryings on of persons who were symbolic of the events and times. And always, I relied on Jim's knowledge of the case, his earlier notes, and the sometimes reluctant and often truncated memory of Collins Catch the Bear himself.

As my research progressed, what emerged was a chronicle of hurt and degradation. Later, long after the case and Collins's death, I knew I was asking readers to accompany me on a painful trek while writing this book. Why should they join me? To put it in another way, why should I, or they, care?

There's something about being human that invites our concern for those who have drawn the short straw in life. Many of the people on the Standing Rock Indian Reservation faced a challenge for survival. This is the story of one of them: Collins Catch the Bear. Derelict or saint? We shall see. It is also the story of trial lawyers who found themselves committed to the defense of a Lakota Sioux charged with the murder of a white man. After the passage of these fleeting years, the cellular question remains: Did we fail?

1.

The available records didn't reveal pretty things. The tribal social worker who occasionally gathered the courage to peer through the door of the shack where Collins Catch the Bear spent his early years described it as "the garbage pit of humanity." Collins's mother, Delilah Catch the Bear, rented the hovel, a single room with a dirt floor that became muddy when the snow melted off the shoes of those who staggered in out of blizzards. The walls of the room, cardboard nailed to two-by-fours, were broken through along the base, and the shack had no electricity, no running water, no beds, and of course no toilet. A small woodstove in the corner pretended to heat the room, but it was warmed mostly by the bodies that occupied it.

In one social worker's report of his visit, a tall, skinny Indian man lay sprawled on the floor. Two other men, dirty and silent, were propped up against a wall. At the other end of the shack, two more men sat with wine bottles clutched in their hands. They appeared stiff and frozen. The social worker reported that empty tin cans, discarded wine bottles, and an assortment of beer cans had been kicked into a corner. The children, partially naked, huddled together next to the stove, their long hair matted and their faces as pale as featherless birds.

On the Standing Rock Indian Reservation in South Dakota the temperature can drop below zero—how low depends on the whims of winter. The U.S. government provided Delilah with "commodities." Most of the food (cans of beans and hash but no fresh fruit or vegetables) was usually devoured the first day. The remainder, if any, was often traded for a dollar bottle of wine, and the children went hungry.

The social worker reported that Delilah sat next to the stove with her children, who seemed unconscious, including two-year-old Collins. Delilah's eyes were open but lifeless. She did not speak. Her skin was gray. She wore what appeared to be an old khaki army jacket whose pockets had been ripped out. The cloth of her pants was too dirty to be identified, and on her sockless feet she wore a pair of old black canvas shoes. A series of scabbed-over sores dotted both her ankles. Her long hair was knotted and tangled, and her face too puffy for her Indian features to prevail.

The records told us that in her eighteenth year, Delilah had had a child by a previous coupling, but the records did not reveal the whereabouts of that child. In 1965, the tribal judge ordered Collins Catch the Bear and the three older Catch the Bear children into foster care. Collins was three. We know little about that placement, but soon Delilah was begging the tribal judge to return her children. She vowed to conquer her alcohol addiction, and after her endless pleas and wailings, Collins and the other Catch the Bear children were returned to her. Then she added yet another child to the family, a girl.

The tribal social worker ordered Delilah to keep the drunks out of the house. He pointed to five men sitting around the shack.

"I can't keep 'em out," Delilah told him. "They just bust the door."

"Put a lock on the door," the social worker said.

"Ain't got no money for locks. Ain't got no hammer."

"Tell the landlord, then."

"He don't do nothin' for me. Says I gotta get out."

"Have you paid your rent?"

She didn't answer.

The social worker pulled out his notebook and began jotting things down. He asked again. "Have you paid your rent?"

"I don't know."

"You didn't pay your rent, did you?"

"Them guys took my money," she said. She motioned to the drunks sitting on the floor.

"Why didn't you report this to us?" the social worker asked.

"Ain't got no phone."

The social worker surveyed the drunks. "Which one took the money?"

"That one over there, that Tom."

"I'm going to have the Indian Police throw them all in jail."

"No," Delilah said. The baby made a small noise, and she slowly pulled out a breast. "Them guys don't let the landlord kick me out. They say they'll kill the landlord if he kicks me out. We ain't got no other place to go."

The social worker said he was going to write up the situation—this lone woman and her children prey to a gang of single men. The men had no jobs, no housing. They could put in an application to the Bureau of Indian Affairs for general assistance, but an applicant had to gather three letters proving he'd tried to get work, and a man could starve or freeze to death before wrangling three such letters. And after going through all that, he'd get only sixty-seven dollars a month in assistance.

The motivation for a hopeless alcoholic's next breath was

somehow to survive long enough for another drink. And the tribal ethic of sharing with a fellow member was often detrimental to any prospect of recovery.

A number of studies have reported the staggeringly high incidence of alcoholism among Native Americans compared to the U.S. population as a whole. One such work, reported in the National Academy of Sciences during a time relevant to our case, found that among the Standing Rock Sioux, "nearly one of every three Indians over 15 years of age drank to excess." The study concluded that the incidence of alcoholism among Indians was more than double that of the white comparison sample; that drinking by Indian youth and women was increasing substantially; and that among young Indian adults (especially males), the incidence of excessive drinking was close to 100 percent.*

On July 31, 1968, the tribal social worker reported that Delilah Catch the Bear had given birth to her seventh child, a girl. Delilah was twenty-nine years old and was receiving $103 a month in assistance. The family was living in the same shack along with the usual assortment of single men who found shelter there.

"I quit drinking," Delilah had told the social worker when he made his previous visit.

"Yeah, I know." The social worker had said. "You quit when all the wine's gone and the money's gone, and you've sold everything you've got." He'd heard the month before that she had tried to hock a pair of her kid's shoes for a dollar, the going price for the cheapest bottle of wine.

"It isn't that she doesn't love her kids," the social worker said. "She doesn't know her kids. She's been drunk for almost twenty years now, and she's only twenty-nine. She'll never make it another year. She hardly knows her kids' names. She'd sell 'em—not

---

* J. O. Whitaker, "Alcohol and the Standing Rock Sioux Tribe: A Twenty-Year Follow-up Study," *Journal of Studies on Alcohol* 43, no. 3 (1982–83), https://trid.trb.org/view/187551.

because she doesn't love 'em—but because she's got the disease. Makes you want to cry. She's not a bad woman. She's just not a human being anymore. Just an organism with a terrible disease. She needs a drink worse than she needs to breathe. Can't think without a drink, and if she has a drink[,] she can't think either. Can't quit if you can't think," the social worker said.

"These kids are dirty," he told Delilah. "When was the last time you gave them a bath?" Delilah didn't answer. The social worker knew better than to ask the question. You don't bathe kids in a creek in wintertime.

"These kids got lice," he said as he inspected the head of the small boy sitting on the floor. "These kids are filthy, and they're sick, and they're suffering from malnutrition. What are you going to do about it, Delilah?"

"I ain't got no money," she said.

"When you get money, you spend it on wine."

"Them guys took my money," she said again.

The young social worker had studied hard in school, and he cared. He knew that if a person could get the "right dynamic" going—well, the "right dynamic" could change things. He'd find her husband, Clayton Catch the Bear, and he'd put him in the shack with Delilah and her kids. Maybe the husband would run the other drunks out.

The social worker found Clayton Catch the Bear drunk and living in an old car body in Mobridge, South Dakota. The social worker vowed to get that right dynamic going, to reunite the husband and his wife, and he took an Indian Police officer along with him in case of trouble.

"I ain't botherin' nobody," Clayton said when the police officer pulled him out of the car body. "I ain't botherin' nobody," he said again. It had become an unwritten law in Mobridge that if an Indian wasn't bothering anyone, he'd be left alone.

"You're comin' with us," the officer said. Then he and the social worker drove Clayton Catch the Bear to Delilah's shack.

He protested all the way: "I wasn't botherin' nobody."

When they arrived, the social worker, with the help of the police officer, shoved Clayton through the door of the shack. "Now, take a look at that," the social worker said. As always, half a dozen drunks were sitting on the floor. The kids were milling around aimlessly. The place stank of urine and wine.

Clayton surveyed the scene with a serious look on his face, swaying slowly back and forth. "I ain't drunk," he said.

"I know," the social worker said, "but you stay right here and sober up and get this mess cleaned up. If you don't stay here, we'll send you to jail." The social worker turned to the police officer for confirmation, "Isn't that right?"

The officer nodded, and then the social worker slammed the door shut and left Clayton Catch the Bear to get things straightened out.

The next month, the social worker reported that he couldn't believe what he'd seen. The drunks were gone! Clayton was there with Delilah and the kids. They were both drunk, but the social worker thought he was making progress. He had to congratulate himself. Now, to get the kids fed and the family on its feet. So, he went to his supervisor for a little help.

"I got the right dynamic going out there," he proudly told his supervisor. "The situation the month before was on the brink of urgent."

"On the brink of urgent, huh?" the supervisor said with a small smile. "I like that. 'On the brink of urgent.' That's a good term. We should use that."

"Well, these drunks had taken over. They'd taken Delilah's money. She was their captive. And the only thing they furnished was a sort of protection against the landlord when the rent came due—sorta like the Mafia. The Indian Mafia," the young man said seriously.

"The Indian Mafia," the supervisor repeated. "That's a good one, too. You're full of good terms. You're gonna do all right here," the supervisor said.

The social worker continued: "It was a flophouse for those drunken singles who had no other place to stay. But I got that straightened out. I brought the husband home, got the right dynamic going. The husband ran the drunks off. We need to build on that dynamic."

"Good," the supervisor said. "Now what?"

"Well, that's what I wanted to talk to you about. I wanted your advice," the young man said.

"I see," the supervisor said. He picked up the social worker's report. "I see there's been seven kids there and two adults, and I see that Delilah's little sister is living there, too, now. What about the money?"

"Well, this is what I wanted to talk to you about. With this right dynamic going and everything, couldn't we find that this is an emergency?"

"This isn't an emergency," the supervisor said. "This is just everyday Indian welfare, and you know it as well as I do. And now that Clayton is home, there's nothing we can do. According to the regs, when both husband and wife live in the same household and both are able-bodied, the payments for the kids stop."

"I know," the young social worker said. "But I figured that in this one special case, we could sorta bend the rule a little to protect the dynamic I got going."

"No, son," the supervisor said. "Rules are rules. Change 'em for you, and we change 'em for everybody. Gotta follow the rules. Go get Clayton a job."

"There aren't any jobs," the social worker said. Then the supervisor put his face in another file, and the young man knew that the interview was over.

Three months later, the social worker petitioned the tribal court to remove the children from Delilah and Clayton Catch the Bear. He told the tribal judge, "We need an order to take custody of the children. The kids are suffering from malnutrition. The kids are hungry. And dirty. I'm not trying to give the Indians a bad name, but by and large, that's the way it is on the rez. They sell their commodities for a bottle. They sell their clothes. They sell every possession they can get their hands on for a drink. And they suffer from every ailment known to mankind—but mostly it's brought on by alcohol. There is no cure for it. It is a disease."

Delilah and her children were finally evicted from the shack in June 1968. On the tenth of July, she was seen with her children living in an old car body along the creek. With no other choice, the young social worker petitioned a trial judge for an order to take custody of the children. His words appear on the record:

> Reports have come to us that Delilah Catch The Bear has been seen drunk carrying her baby on her hip down the streets of Mobridge with the other children following. The last report advised that she had returned to the reservation but we have not yet located her.
>
> Mr. and Mrs. Catch The Bear have demonstrated on numerous occasions in the past that they are not able to provide a suitable home for their children. Their present conduct is such that the children are suffering neglect both physically and emotionally. We recommend the removal of these children from their parents if they are not able to show a change in their behavior within sixty days.

"Okay," the tribal judge said to the young social worker when the sixty days had elapsed and no change had been observed in the behavior of either Delilah or Clayton Catch the Bear and the well-being of the neglected, malnourished children was at stake. "You make 'er up [the order] and I'll sign 'er." Later, a hearing was set, and at the time of the hearing, no one in the courtroom by the name of "Catch the Bear" responded. Clayton and Delilah were no-shows. So, the judge signed the papers the social worker had laid in front of him. Delilah was too drunk to kiss her babies good-bye.

2.

The Social Services Department of the Bureau of Indian Affairs deposited the two Catch the Bear boys, Anthony, age six, and Collins, five, with Donald and Virginia McClain of McLaughlin, South Dakota. The McClains were an exemplary white Catholic couple with two older boys of their own. The BIA would pay them a monthly stipend for care of the boys, though two more little children in the family wouldn't cost much more.

I talked with the McClains. Mrs. McClain, a mother to her core, was proud that her home had been approved by the U.S. government to provide foster care for Indian children. Her husband, Donald, was a construction foreman on the railroad. He said he liked kids, but he wasn't home much; he had to be on the road. Mrs. McClain recalls the day Anthony and Collins arrived at her house.

"Look at them," Mrs. McClain said after the social worker had delivered Anthony and Collins. "Aren't they a sight?" She reported that she tried to kiss little Collins, the boy with the fat baby cheeks and the skinny legs that came out of his body like sticks out of a bloated bladder. "My, my," she said. "This is not a very friendly little boy. But he will learn to be a good boy. Good boys grow in good homes."

"Probably never had any parental guidance at all," Mr. McClain said. "Maybe got 'em just in time. Hope it isn't too late."

Collins had "the prettiest black eyes," Mrs. McClain said. "But look at him. He looks like a scared rabbit." She laughed affectionately and scrubbed the naked little boy down with soap and a washcloth.

"Probably never had soap on 'em before," Mr. McClain said.

"Did the little Catch the Bear ever have soap on him before?" Mrs. McClain asked in sweet baby talk, but the child began to cry, and Anthony, his older brother, began to cry, and in unison they were like two coyote pups howling in the night.

"They're probably lonesome for their mother," Mrs. McClain said, grabbing Collins and trying to hug him again, but he kicked and screamed like a freshly captured little animal. She told us he was screaming so loudly and gasping for air so violently that she was afraid for the child. When she put him down, the boy ran naked to the corner, sobbing and shivering. Mrs. McClain put a big towel around him.

"Gonna be like raising a couple of pet coons," Mr. McClain said, shaking his head.

The two McClain boys were watching at the bathroom door, grinning and pointing and snickering to each other. "Looky, ain't they cute," the older boy said. "Ain't they just cute as little monkeys?"

"That's right," Mrs. McClain said. "They are sweet, dear little Indian children, and they've come to live with us."

"Where's their mama?" the oldest boy asked.

"Their mother was a drunk, and so was their father, and that's why we send you to church, so that you will learn how to live right. These little children have never been to church like you." Mrs. McClain smiled at her own darling boys and kissed them both.

"And I will give these two little boys, Collins and Anthony, kisses, too. We will treat everybody the same in this house," she said, and she reached over to kiss Collins, but he lowered his head and began to cry again and shook her off with his bony little shoulders.

Then Mrs. McClain dressed the children. She bought new shoes for the boys, and there were certain hand-me-downs from the older McClain children that should not go to waste. "'Waste not, want not,' the Bible says."

Mr. McClain said that, later on, he saw the kids scratching their heads, and sure enough, there were body lice all right, plain as day, and they had to shave the boys' heads. "I've seen it before," he said. "Hungry children always seem to be supper for hungry lice."

"These Indians! I don't understand them," Virginia McClain said the next day. "Letting those little children go hungry like that. They ate like starved little animals. I had to stop them. This boy," she pointed to Collins, "drank two tall glasses of milk and wanted more. I thought he'd get sick for sure. But he won't touch the Wheaties."

"Never ate decent food," Mr. McClain said.

"I cooked them up a bowl of oatmeal and put sugar and milk on it, and the boy"—she pointed to Collins again—"burned himself, he ate it so fast. Never had a dish of cooked oatmeal in his life, I bet. Probably never even had a decent hot meal. When I opened the icebox, he looked in, and the first thing he saw that he recognized was a weenie. He was so cute. There was fruit there, apples and oranges, but the first thing he grabbed was a weenie."

"Probably all he ate at home—if he ate at all, Mr. McClain said. "There's sure not much profit in it, but it's something for the missus to do while I'm gone during the week. She loves children; reminds me of Old Mother Hubbard. Besides, people need somethin' to do with their lives."

Mrs. McClain nodded her agreement.

"We'll get 'em straightened out right away," Mr. McClain said to his wife. "Here, you kids quit staring at these little boys. Go play with them now," he said to his own two sons. But when the youngest McClain boy pulled him by the hand, Collins held on to the chair and began to cry again.

Collins and Anthony were always tight in the McClain household. In some ways, they banded together against the McClain children, which isn't to say the two little boys were mean, but they hung together the way animals of the same species do. They ate together and slept together, and if they got separated, they'd cry. Mrs. McClain took the boys everywhere she took her own, and they got everything her own children got, but the Indian boys knew they didn't belong.

"One time I was helping Collins read," Mrs. McClain said. "He loved to read. Learned to read very easily, easier maybe than my own, and I asked Collins, 'Do you like Dick and Jane?'

"'No,' he said.

"I was surprised. 'Why don't you like Dick and Jane?'

"'Because they're not Indians,' he said. Then I said, 'Well, don't you even like Spot?' And he said, 'No.' And I said, 'Why don't you like little Spot?' And Collins said, 'I don't like Spot because he is not an Indian dog.' And I didn't say anything more. I just let it go by."

Virginia McClain said she loved Collins. But he knew he was not white. He knew his mother had discarded him like an empty bottle of wine. He knew he wasn't blood kin of the McClain's. He was Lakota, but could not speak Lakota. Some of the kids at school called him nigger. He didn't once hear from his mother, or from any of his blood. He didn't call Mrs. McClain Mother. He knew the tribal judge could take him from the McClains whenever he pleased, like emptying the garbage into another pail.

The next year, the tribal authorities sent Anthony back to the reservation to live with an aunt who wanted him. "That was very hard on poor Collins, to lose his big brother," Mrs. McClain said.

"I tried to comfort him. He cried. He wouldn't eat. He wouldn't talk. I worried about him. He was grieving. At night, he would cry out in his sleep. He cried every night for weeks, and it was such a frightening loud, wailing cry.

"He wouldn't eat. He sat at the table, turned his head from the food, and if we said, 'Collins, now eat your food, honey,' he would only cry. He wouldn't let me hold him, like his whole body was burned or something, like touching him was too painful for him to bear. I thought he would die. I called the social worker and told him, but he said there was nothing they could do about it. The aunt who took Anthony had that right.

"Collins wasn't an affectionate child," Mrs. McClain said. "But we had long talks together, and he told me things. He told me he knew that his mother must not love him, or she wouldn't have let him go, and I think after they took Anthony away like that, that Collins thought there was something wrong with him. 'Why didn't my aunt take me?' he asked me once. It only came up once," Mrs. McClain said, "I tried to answer him as best I could. 'Well, she had children of her own, Collins. She only had room for one more.'

"'Why did she take Anthony?' he asked me.

"'Maybe he was the oldest. I don't know,' I said. What do you tell a child why somebody chose his brother over him? I didn't know what to say, so we didn't talk about it after that."

Mrs. McClain said Collins did well in school at McLaughlin. "He learned fast, read well. But he stayed to himself, and never brought anybody home. He had no playmates. He was a lonely child. He seemed to bring it on himself, and he tried not to cry, but if somebody corrected him or said hardly anything to him at all, he would start crying. He was very sensitive." It got so that the McClains sort of let him alone. It was easier that way.

In 1972, the McClains moved to Milwaukee, and of course Collins moved with them. He was ten. He attended the Blakewood Grade School and did well there at first, but the children teased him about his name. "Did you catch the bear? What did you do with the bear?" They taunted him over and over in their singsong child's voices. And at night he cried out in his sleep.

To be able to take Collins to Milwaukee with them, Mrs. McClain signed a document required by the tribal court. It acknowledged that Collins was in their "temporary custody," and that the McClains would "cooperate with the Court and return Collins when the Court so orders."

Collins knew he belonged not to the McClains but to the tribal judge, with his far-reaching power that could extend clear to Milwaukee. He belonged to forces in the Bureau of Indian Affairs he did not know, not by sight, nor by name, forces with the power of God, but a god who cared only about the records kept by the BIA.

3.

Over the passing years, Collins never heard from his mother; nor she from him. His father, of course, had been the bearer of only the seed and the name. The records reveal that Delilah died in 1976. She was thirty-seven years old. Collins was fourteen. He was not informed of her death. By then, she'd given birth to eight surviving children and probably died of acute alcoholism. Where she died, the details of her death, and where she was buried were not of sufficient importance to win a place in the official files. The whereabouts of Clayton, Collins's father, if indeed he was still alive, were unknown.

Mrs. McClain wrote the tribal court that Collins was doing fine. She thought it "very good" that the child should be away from the influences of the reservation and learn to live "in larger places." It seemed not to occur to her that Collins might have strong feelings of kinship for his blood relatives and their shared history.

We're all tribal creatures. We become lost in the cities if we do not form a tribe through our work, our churches and clubs, or our neighborhood associations. Without a tribe, we feel abandoned, become alienated, and grow paranoid and sometimes violent. We hover over our smartphone screens and accept certain television personalities as our tribal members. When more than ninety thousand people pay hard-earned dollars for a seat at a football game to watch their team in battle, and millions of others are nailed to their screens hooting, we are watching the tribal gene at work. Perhaps on a larger, more dangerous scale, the tribal gene sends thousands as a national tribe to kill thousands of foreign tribal members in needless tribal wars.

Collins had been wrested from his tribal origins and dropped in among the bulging multitudes in a large city. His potential friends were all white. Like a tiny lost bird in a flock of gulls, he was worse than alone. He was physically part of the McClain family, who claimed he belonged to them, yet he knew he did not belong to them. He belonged to the tribal judge, whoever he was. And the tribal judge could send him whenever he decreed.

And love? Yes, the McClains were well-meaning people. But how could they love him? He was not of their blood. Theirs was an imposed love, and such a love jeered in his ears. Then came loneliness, then despair, and then a compulsion to run. *To run.* Anywhere. And Collins ran, ending up on the reservation.

Fourteen is a bad age for boys. I remember. At fourteen, I was taken over by the predictable psychosis of puberty. Reason is a trespasser to the adolescent. During adolescence, parental love is tested. I look back on that wretched period with regret—and with admiration for my parents, who endured nature's assault on me, and mine on them. I would follow no rules. I respected no adult, all of whom I believed infinitely stupid. Yet, through it all, I knew I was taking advantage of suffering parents who still loved me, not because I was loveable, but because I belonged to them.

In September 1976, the tribal judge placed Collins in the Community School on the reservation, where he was housed in the students' dormitory. He refused to study; he ran away. He was caught, brought back, and endured a "behavior modification program"—whatever that entailed, providing him with the latest proof that he was worthless unless transformed by force into someone acceptable to those in power.

The Community School records report that "he roams around at night, and he is suspected as being involved in breaking into a school building." The school's social worker claimed that Collins was extremely hostile, and when the social worker talked to him, the boy often cried. The social worker confessed, "Part of his trouble may be that he was enrolled in the 8th grade, but upon reviewing his transcripts it was found that he was supposed to be in the 7th."

I doubt that Collins had trouble keeping up with any eighth-grade curriculum. What he, an already small Indian boy, would have found challenging was being carelessly chucked in with kids physically a year older than he. It was like putting a puppy in with a pack of older, bigger dogs that would chew him up. Even the American Society for the Prevention of Cruelty to Animals would have condemned that.

In November 1976, the reservation social worker wrote that "Collins' behavior continues to deteriorate." He reportedly pulled a knife on another student. As punishment, he was kicked out of the dorms and lodged in jail with the drunks. When he got out, he set a couple of fires down by the river and was thrown back in jail. He got into fights. He ran away in the middle of the night, and that sent law enforcement on his tail again.

Upon his capture, the tribal judge ordered Collins to the mental hospital in Jamestown, North Dakota, where the boy found himself locked in with "a bunch of crazies." Collins must have asked himself, Am I crazy like them? A psychiatrist there concluded that he suffered from a "behavior disorder of childhood with unsocialized aggressive reaction, moderate to severe"—in short, this fourteen-year-old boy was pissed to the max.

The doctor recommended that the hospital keep Collins, further evaluate him, "and treat him psychologically and psychosocially and educationally," whatever that meant. No one suggested that the boy be cared for in a sensitive, loving way as a lonely, frightened human.

A month later, still at the hospital in Jamestown, Collins began expressing a desire to return to the McClains. The doctor wanted to keep him, for what purpose he didn't reveal. Another month later, he was sent back to the reservation with the original diagnosis and discharged to the tribal judge "for further disposition." Easy word, *disposition*. Among other things, it means "the act of disposing of."

Mrs. McClain tells us the story in her November 1976 letter to the tribal judge:

> I find it impossible to believe that Collins would deliberately set fire to destroy something. As for his possession of a knife[,] he would have to be extremely provoked to threaten someone with it. I feel very much at fault for what has happened because maybe I have overly protected Collins . . . but he was always the smallest boy. He always took the blame and punishment for things that happened at school rather than tell his side of things.

Years later, I would remember Mrs. McClain's last sentence as having been both insightful and frighteningly prophetic—that is, that Collins "always took the blame and punishment."

Mrs. McClain's letter continued:

> Collins came [upon] a boy who had a small 4th grade boy on the floor[,] kicking him[,] and the [fourth-grade] boy was crying. Collins' reaction was pulling the [aggressor] boy off and hitting him. The principal punished Col-

lins—made him eat his lunch in the school garage[,] where it was cold and dirty[,] and said he should mind his own business.

We do not know if the Indian judge read her letter, but I could just imagine the authorities at the school as they talked about "the Catch the Bear situation."

Waste of time, the principal might have said.

When Collins was suspended for cutting a class, Mrs. McClain was told that he "was wasting the teacher's time and the taxpayer's money."

I've never seen a single page in the Bureau of Indian Affairs records (or any other record purporting to reflect the life of Collins Catch the Bear) that recounted Collins's loneliness; his deep yearning for his own tribe; his sense of abandonment; or the feeling of worthlessness that set in when the surrounding world proclaimed he was worthless.

And no one seemed to understand that Collins also suffered another painful affliction: he was burdened with a higher intelligence than most, and so his teachers unknowingly imposed endless hours of boredom on him in the classroom.

One needs to remember also that the Sioux were a Plains people. They lived for centuries in the wide-open spaces, and the need to roam with the wind and the weather and to follow the buffalo herds was implanted in their blood.

Mrs. McClain's letter to the tribal judge continues:

> He [Collins] is like our own son, but maybe he continues to need more than we can give. It broke our hearts to send him back, but everything we tried failed. Collins had no one who cared for him except us. I certainly hope he knows we are there when he needs us. Every child needs someone for security and love, and Collins needs that right now. I can imagine how lost and alone he must

feel being among strangers there and unable to contact anyone. I'm so afraid he may become bitter and resentful from all this and think no one cares, so why should he? He probably feels he is being punished for what he has done, and no one is there to give him the support he needs.

I know this may be unjust to say, but living in that area myself for a number of years[,] I know how hard and mean some of those people can be. I'm very sorry now that we let Collins return to the reservation as the environment there greatly influences a child's character and behavior.

What Mrs. McClain didn't appreciate was that the power embodied in the tribal judge she was addressing has no ears to hear nor heart to care. The subject is reduced to an object. The object is subject to rules and regulations that fill endless pages. And the object is also subject to the whims of those emotionally dormant representatives of power, such as the psychiatrist at the mental hospital who writes away in his deadly professional lexicon, the words empty of the heart.

The question remained: who now would take Collins?

We next see him in June 1977, at the Standing Rock Youth Ranch. He's living in the dorm. The director reports that Collins "is easily upset by seemingly insignificant happenings and sets to crying with little cause. He is hostile and resistive to authority. Collins is quite often very 'mouthy,' and employs the foulest of language. Once Collins is agitated, he is very difficult to calm down. He will 'screech' for a period of a few minutes, then cry for up to two hours." The director had doubts about Collins's suitability for their program.

One of the staff members at the ranch reported seeing Collins walking down by the pasture alone. Thinking he might be going

AWOL, she picked him up in her vehicle and told him to remain in the dormitory. She reported that "he immediately went outside against my wishes."

On the evening of July 20, 1977, Collins ran away from the ranch. The police were called.

On July 24, Mrs. McClain wrote Collins a lovely, newsy letter about the family and their move to La Crosse, Wisconsin. She concluded:

> Collins, be a good boy and don't get into anything. Life is what we make it[,] so make yours a good[,] fulfilling one with a good future ahead. You are a very good person; and very smart[,] so you can go a long way and have a good life if you set your mind to do so.
>
> I think of you many times and have looked for a letter from you but since you haven't written thought I should.
> Love,
> Virginia

For lack of a better address, her letter was sent to the Social Services Office at Fort Yates. It was filed and never delivered to Collins.

At fifteen, Collins was still at the Youth Ranch when he got into a fight instigated by another kid. Collins took after the aggressor with a fireplace poker. The director said that Collins was frequently involved in fighting, running away, huffing, and occasionally smoking. But he was getting better, and she wanted to keep him on the ranch.

Then, one day, Collins and some other boys filled a cigarette with gunpowder. It ended up in the hands of one of the girls. She lit it, and suffered serious burns. The boys ran away, but they were apprehended by the McLaughlin Police, who returned them to the ranch. They were confined to the dormitory for a week as punishment. This was on October 23, 1977. Five days later, the boys ran away again.

The director of the Youth Ranch didn't give up on Collins. Though the boy was aggressive to students and staff alike, "she remained hopeful" and recommended that he stay with them "indefinitely." What we don't see in the reports is what must have been obvious: that Collins had something to offer. He was a lad of high intelligence. He loved to read. He could express himself to a point of eloquence, if he chose. He was refreshingly special. He not only enjoyed a superior intellect, but also bore a superior brand of stubbornness. It was as if he carried an invisible sign on his back: "Do Not Mess with Me. Though I'm Small, I Will Hurt You. Leave Me Alone. And Please, Do Not Bore Me. I Am Not Small in the Mind."

On November 16, 1977, Collins went AWOL again. And again, he encountered the police.

Finally, the director of the youth ranch gave up. She wrote in a report that Collins hated school and wanted to return to the reservation and go to the school in neighboring Wakpala. It was in Wakpala that he'd lived those years of his infancy with his mother in that shack crowded with drunken men. Perhaps, I thought, when I read this, he was still in search of his mother.

Collins was released to an unknown Indian woman in Wakpala identified in the records only as "a friend." In order to stay with her, he was required to earn passing grades at school and stay out of trouble. If he failed this time, all concerned agreed, including Collins, he would be "placed" at the State Industrial School in Mandan, North Dakota, the reform school for bad boys.

His report card at the school in Wakpala barely got him by: He failed math, got a C+ in Art, a D in Social Studies, and a D- in Science. He was absent five and a half days and tardy twice. He got passing marks in "Cooperation," "Courtesy," "Work Habits,"

"Dependability," and "Obedience." He scored a D in "Citizenship," however one might have defined that word. The Wakpala school gave up on him, and the school at Fort Yates refused to take him. Still, somehow, he avoided being sent to the reformatory.

It was now May 28, 1978, and we find Collins in Sky Ranch, South Dakota, where he had somehow wangled his way into the Catholic Sky Ranch for Boys. He is receiving high marks in all subjects, and the school's "learning disability specialist" reports that Collins is "well behaved, quiet, well liked by his peers, is self motivated and should be able to complete high school through Independent High School Correspondence Study Class."

This note also appears in the files: "He has some trouble with poor sportsmanship in basketball. He took any fouls against him personally and yelled at the referees. In baseball[,] he picked a fight with a player from the other team and even chased him back to his bench."

Reading these things, I found myself admiring Collins's courage (and regretting his lack of good judgment).

In October 1978, he ran away from the Sky Ranch for Boys after he was disciplined for undefined offenses. He said his mission was to be with a family that wanted him.

On January 9, 1979, the BIA Social Services Department, having no place to put him, took Collins to court.

No *place*.

Collins protested: "Melda Takes the Hat—she will take care of me," he said, referring to an Indian woman in McLaughlin, South Dakota. He began to cry.

The social worker told the judge, "Melda has called us and told us she doesn't want him in her home. He is detrimental to the family."

"That ain't so," Collins said. "I'm not detrimental. I am *not* detrimental." Then, according to the report, he went on a crying jag.

Finally, the judge couldn't take it any longer. "You call Melda. Ask her again. I'll wait."

The social worker left and soon reported back to the judge. "I called Melda Takes the Hat at McLaughlin, and she said she did not want him around."

Again we see Collins at Standing Rock Youth Ranch. The record from this period is silent, leading us to suspect that the boy's charisma served him well once more and that he was able to convince those in charge that this time he would be a successful inmate. His behavior was reported good for the first month, but in February he was caught smoking marijuana. He was also skipping classes again.

After these chaotic years, someone arranged for Collins to see his father at the Detox Center in Fort Yates, where Clayton had been placed. But when Collins arrived, he found that his father had gone.

In March, Collins was reported as behaving well, except he'd been sniffing plastic wood. His counselor, Charles Walking Elk, said Collins needed someone to talk to about his problems. Maybe he could locate the boy's father. But Walking Elk later reported that he was unable to find Clayton Catch the Bear. He thought he'd fled to someplace in Montana.

In April 1979, Charles Walking Elk reported that Collins had been arrested for being drunk and disorderly and had been sent to jail in Fort Yates. Back at school at the ranch, he attended one class and then skipped school the rest of the day. He was reported drunk again in May and again in June. By July, Collins was asking to leave the ranch. "I'm bored out there. There is nothing to do. I would like to stay with anybody who will take me." Then he ran—where, the record does not reveal.

He was retrieved by the tribal police and brought before the tribal judge. What to do with this boy, this boy with special talents? They're the kind who are often the hardest to deal with, but with such children, the rewards of patience are also greater. The judge again sent Collins to the State Hospital in Jamestown for evaluation. He escaped and, predictably, returned to the reservation, where he was again picked up by the tribal police.

The tribal judge found that Collins was incorrigible and, as a last resort, ordered that he be confined at the State Industrial School in Mandan, North Dakota. The order was signed on September 26, 1979, by Isaac Dog Eagle Jr., associate judge. Collins was seventeen years old.

The records from the State Industrial School are sparse. He was released in June 1981.

Thereafter, Collins was back wandering on the reservation. To obtain financial assistance, he'd furnished the Bureau of Indian Affairs with the requisite three letters showing that he had sought but been refused employment, which qualified him for assistance. He would receive ninety dollars a month. The final notes in his record show him working odd jobs, being fired, and applying for assistance—the standard, well-worn, completely predictable revolving process for many Indian men on the reservation.

World without end.

Amen.

4.

Let us wander for a moment across history to the far-off settlement called Gordon, Nebraska, a pinch of a town that claimed a little more than a thousand souls, about 10 percent of whom were Indians. It was the night of February 12, 1972. (Collins would have been ten years old and living with the McClains.) A couple of white toughs were out looking for trouble, and they'd focused on an Indian who was hiding in a used-car lot. The whites were drinking, and for entertainment they'd decided "to bust the Indian on accounta he has it comin'. I mean, he was messin' up the streets a Gordon with his fuckin' presence, right?"

The Indian's name was Raymond Yellow Thunder. Yellow Thunder, an Oglala Lakota, was one of seven children. In high school he'd been an average student, a good athlete, and known as "the best artist in school." When sober, he worked as a ranch hand. He was the grandson of Chief American Horse, a U.S. Army Indian Scout, statesman, educator, and historian who in the late nineteenth century sought friendship with the whites and education for his people.

On that evening in 1972, the two whites, Leslie and Melvin Hare, entertained themselves by beating and kicking the unarmed Yellow Thunder into unconsciousness. They then stuffed him in the trunk of their car, drove around Gordon, and finally, as the climax of their adventure, pulled off his pants and shoved the half-naked Yellow Thunder into the American Legion Hall, where a party was in progress. Somehow, he got to the police station and asked for a cell to pass the night. Eight days later, his lifeless body was found in an old wrecked car.

An autopsy revealed that Yellow Thunder had died of a "subdural hematoma, caused by blunt trauma to his forehead above his right eye." Possibly where he'd been kicked in the head when he was down.

The local authorities arrested the white men, but they were released on a $625 bond pending trial.

Good boys, the folks said. *Everybody knows 'em. Not goin' anyplace. Charged 'em with manslaughter. Murder wasn't in the cards. After all, there was no intent to kill, right? Just a little merriment. A little fun. Boys got a little rough, you had to admit. But boys will be boys. It wasn't like there was a murder with premeditation and all.*

Leslie and Melvin Hare were tried by a jury and found guilty of false imprisonment and manslaughter. Leslie Hare was sentenced to six years with a $500 fine, and Melvin, apparently because of his lesser involvement in the death, to two years with a $500 fine. Their convictions were affirmed by the Nebraska Supreme Court. I don't know how much prison time they actually served.

The Yellow Thunder family had earlier petitioned the American Indian Movement, a segment of which had been established at the Pine Ridge Indian Reservation in South Dakota. AIM responded with its red flags and its drums and two hundred cars that drove from Pine Ridge to Gordon, Nebraska, where a large force of sheriff's deputies, state troopers, and FBI agents met them. The Gordon community got riled up and jumpy. No assaults or killings occurred, but businesses were fearful that the Indians would boycott Gordon and cause more trouble. This demonstration seemed to conclude AIM's response to the beating death of Raymond Yellow Thunder at Gordon.

But Raymond Yellow Thunder had not been forgotten. On April 4, 1981, members of AIM drove a small caravan of cars to a sacred place in the Black Hills of South Dakota about twelve miles southwest of Rapid City and set up camp within the boundaries of the National Forest, a place henceforth to be known as Yellow Thunder Camp, in memory of Raymond Yellow Thunder. The Indians who established the camp erected their tepees at the base of a cliff, by good water that ran pure and clear through the tall pines. The Indians claimed eight hundred of the millions of acres that made up what the Sioux called the Paha Sapa (loosely translated as the Black Hills), all of which had been signed over to the Sioux by the 1868 Treaty of Fort Laramie. The Means brothers Russell and Bill and the spiritual leader Mathew King said the camp was perfectly lawful any way you cut it. To the director of the Black Hills National Forest, James Mathers, the Indians were trespassers, plain and simple. The Indians' response to Mathers: "How can we be trespassers by occupying our own lands?"

Groups often applied to the U.S. Forest Service for parcels of land in the National Forest upon which to build churches, schools, and other facilities. The Boy Scouts and Girl Scouts had had no trouble obtaining the necessary acres for their camps, and church groups and universities had permanent sites within the boundaries of the National Forests. AIM's leaders were no different: like good, God-fearing citizens, they later made appropriate application to the U.S. Forest Service for a permit to occupy those eight hundred sacred acres in the Paha Sapa permanently.

"The youth," the Yellow Thunder Camp's application recited, "will be educated to the environment of the hills; the people will live in the sacred manner in relation to the environment, which is, in the very real sense, the Lakota church."

Russell Means said, "We want Yellow Thunder to be an example to all on reservations. We want to show the world there is an alternative to the industrial based society."

By noon, maybe fifty persons, mostly Lakota Sioux, had moved into the area and started setting up their tents and tepees. By dark, two tepees were up and bark was being stripped from freshly cut lodgepole pine for a third. A small group of men and women were talking softly. A cold wind drove wet snowflakes into their faces, but the children were laughing and playing in one of the tepees.

As the Indians set up their camp, the sounds of their labor echoed from the granite canyon walls across the way. But the people there were afraid. They waited, huddled in blankets, fearful that the authorities would come to arrest them. By dark, a canvas-covered sweat lodge had been thrown up, and inside, by the sweat of their bodies, Indian men sent out their prayers to the Great Spirit.

Their prayers were met by the words of Director Mathers of the Black Hills National Forest when he told the *Rapid City Journal*, "There is plenty of legal muscle and factual muscle. I mean there's plenty of law enforcement to evict them very quickly. That is a fact," he said.

Sheriff Mel Larson, up for reelection the following year, conferred with the FBI. At some point, two vans loaded with heavily armed Bureau agents showed up at the camp's newly established gate.

"What's your business?" the Indians asked.

"Turkey hunting," the federal agents said.

Later, the Indians reported seeing the armed agents in camouflage prowling on the ridge above the camp in the surrounding pines.

Most of the white people in Rapid City thought the Yellow Thunder Camp was an out-and-out takeover by AIM of eight hundred acres of National Forest, and they were up in arms.

By the middle of August, the Forest Service was out of administrative patience, and the Indians were given until September to vacate the premises. Mathers of the Forest Service said, "The biggest concern, aside from the fact that AIM's occupation of the 800 acres violates the Forest Service's policy of multiple use and instead turns it into a single use for only Indians, is that the public is excluded from those 800 acres."

"Got any weapons out there?" a reporter from the *Rapid City Journal* asked Russell Means, one of the camp's founders.

"If I told you, I'd probably be talking to you from the witness stand," Means replied. "We don't lay all of our cards on the table at one time."

An Interior Department spokesman said, "Freeze 'em out. Come winter they'll be hightailin' it with the first snowflake. Forest has a way of taking care of a lot of problems."

Russell Means predicted bloodshed if the government tried to eject them. "If we are forced to defend the camp there will be a holocaust." And so, the tension mounted, and the camp's occupants dug in.

In their application for a permit, the Indians employed the technical language of grant seekers that the government would understand: "The Black Hills region of the contemporary state of South Dakota is and has been central to Lakota spirituality; Lakota spirituality requires, as an integral aspect of itself, unhampered access to and occupancy of the Black Hills—the Jerusalem of the Lakota religion—the Lakota spirituality cannot be divorced from this day-to-day life in the Black Hills, for the Lakota believes man does not own the land." Man is part of the earth. If there be ownership, the earth owns him.

The application then asked: "Does the Lakota possess the inherent national right to perpetuate itself—to retain the integrity of its spiritual existence—or will the United States Government knowingly engage in a policy of overt cultural genocide at this historical juncture?"

The people at Yellow Thunder Camp waited for a raid by the U.S. Marshals and the sheriff's officers. But no attack came. Instead, Forest Service officials arrived at about eleven o'clock one morning, inspected the camp, and demanded that the Indians obtain permits for their two open campfires, one for the kitchen and the other for the sweat lodge. Then the Forest Service men sat the camp leaders down and instructed them on how to manage the fires so as to prevent their spreading, speaking to them as they might speak to children, and advised them to get portable toilets, which the camp occupants said they would gladly do, provided they could raise the money.

Then Frank Fools Crow, a holy man from the Oglala Sioux, came to the camp. Fools Crow gave the camp occupants his blessing, smoked the pipe with them, and encouraged them in their endeavor. The Lakota AIM announced a powwow for the coming Saturday and invited their brothers and sisters from the various Indian nations to come bless them and support them in this new mission for the American Indian. The Oglala Sioux Tribal Council voted 28 to 5 to oppose the Yellow Thunder occupation. But an elder, James Holy Eagle, quoted from the sayings of Sitting Bull: "We must use our voices together like a weapon. We will continue to live as Indians now that we are back in our country. The Black Hills were given to the Lakota by the Great Spirit."

The *Rapid City Journal* reported a "new kind of Indian" at the Lakota AIM camp. "Preferring permits to bullets, a more mellow and cagier American Indian Movement is trying to beat the federal government at its own game. They have consciously followed the letter and intent of the law and the Forest Service regulations, and even James Mathers, the Forest Supervisor, had to admit that 'if everybody in the National Forest was that cooperative it would be great.'"

But, the *Journal* reported, Mathers and other officials also said that the Lakota AIM "are backed by high-powered lawyers, and are trying to create national precedents. They know their rights." He continued: "They are playing a waiting game trying to test the administrative procedure to its limit." Then Mathers said that the Yellow Thunder Camp would get no permanent permit. "We will treat them like any other camper."

Though the camp's occupants waited for an attack, the federal government turned to the courts rather than to force, filing a suit against the Indians and asking a federal judge to order them off the National Forest land. Still, Bruce Ellison, a lawyer for the Yellow Thunder Camp, believed that an overt attack of physical force was coming from someplace, and he filed an affidavit in court supporting this belief.

Ellison claimed that the U.S. Marshals had photographed the camp, that maps had been prepared, and that a special group of marshals had just finished a two-week training exercise specially designed to take out the Yellow Thunder Camp. According to Ellison, U.S. marshal Robert Leighton had told him, "Seizing the camp is not going to be a seventy-one-day, Wounded Knee–type operation. It'll be over in thirty minutes." The training of the marshals was supposedly so vigorous that some marshals, playing the camp's defenders in mock battles, suffered serious injuries—one, a broken leg; and another, a wound requiring seventeen stitches. The U.S. Marshals denied that there was any plan for an attack on the camp.

When the deep freeze of winter set in, the Indians put stoves in their tepees fashioned from fifty-five-gallon oil drums, to which they attached stovepipes that extended up through the teepees' canvas. They then piled dirt over plastic liners around the edges of the tepees, to keep out the cold and snow. They thought they could make it through the winter as their ancestors had. "We're gonna make it all right," they said. It was one of the coldest winters in years. "We're gonna make it. The spirit of Yellow Thunder is here."

Bill Means, one of the founders of Yellow Thunder Camp, said, "We're building an image of perseverance. We're gonna stay."

And they stayed—and made it through the winter.

The press published supportive articles. "AIM is playing the game—and playing it well—and the camp is gaining a legitimacy that surprises even the camp founders themselves." With the future of Yellow Thunder in the hands of the federal courts as well as the spirits, the camp needed a good image, and such positive coverage could sway the federal judge deciding whether the Indians could stay.

But some local folks claimed they knew the truth about AIM. All that business about peace and regaining the Indian ways was just so much propaganda for the liberal press. AIM hadn't changed. It was still the same bunch of troublemakers born of that seventy-one-day standoff in 1973 at Wounded Knee, where two Indians were killed and a U.S. marshal was shot and paralyzed.

No record reveals exactly when Collins Catch the Bear joined the Lakota Sioux at the Yellow Thunder Camp, but we know he was there on July 21, 1982, the day the white man Clarence Tollefson was shot dead. And that changed everything.

5.

Tollefsen had been up on the ridge overlooking the Yellow Thunder Camp. He'd exited his pickup camper, walked to the cliff's edge, and stood staring down at the camp. The camp now comprised nearly twenty tepees, their canvas stretched over long, slender lodgepole pine, its rough, dark bark peeled off with the white man's drawknife. The white man's canvas had turned sooty over the winter from the smoke of the burning pine wood. When the lazy late-morning summer breeze shifted slightly, the sound from a rock-and-roll radio station drifted up to the ridge.

The Indian women were hanging out the wash on cotton clotheslines strung between tall pines, and half-naked children were playing in a small stream, running in and out of open tepee flaps, laughing and hopping into the sun. The children crawled in under the legs of the Indian women and then went splashing wildly into the patient creek, shouting to one another and making gleeful sounds.

Except for the barren walls of the cliff, the surrounding hills were covered with pines so dense and so dark green that from afar they looked black—hence the Lakota name the Paha Sapa, or the white man's name the Black Hills.

On the forest floor, sparse grass fought for sunlight, growing tall and thin, and on the edges of the timber, the arrowroot balsam and the blue lupine had already bloomed and wilted in the heat of summer. The cloudless sky was a pale blue, almost gray, and longed for the early evening hours. At that point, the massive cumulus clouds would create towering mountains of billowing white. And later, explosions of lightning and thunder would announce scattered, cooling showers.

Down a way, the creek had been backed up behind boulders that formed a long, narrow pond constructed by the farmers below, hoping to capture irrigation waters—Victoria Lake, they called it. Green algae grew along the pond's edge, and in the heat of the day, the croaking frogs were muted.

On the cliff side of the dam, a metal, boxlike contraption held up on two-by-fours rose about eight feet high. A hose extended from the bottom of the box to provide the Indians with sun-warmed water for homemade showers. Below the dam was a small garden with crooked rows of vegetables growing in various shades of green.

On the opposite side of the canyon squatted the security shack, a makeshift affair of old boards and tarpaper, and a single pole across the road served as a gate. A wooden arrowhead had been nailed to one end of the pole and wooden feathers to the other, so that the gate resembled a gigantic arrow. The gate was raised and lowered by hand with the aid of a rope and pulley. A congregation of skinny mouse-gray dogs and their skinny half-grown pups lay in the shade of the security shack.

Across the way was parked an ancient red Dodge flatbed truck. The truck's hood was up, like an old man who'd died with his mouth locked open. All four of its tires were flat, and rust showed through its gray undercoat.

Witnesses claimed that the killing of the white man, Tollefson, occurred just past noon, maybe as late as twelve thirty, that Wednesday. Somebody from the Yellow Thunder Camp had driven to the telephone booth at the fire station five miles down the road and called the Sheriff's Office. The officer's report showed that the call came in at 2:51 in the afternoon. The report stated that an Indian-sounding male had called requesting that a deputy come to the camp right away. A white man had just killed himself. And when the sheriff's dispatcher asked the name of the calling party, it sounded like "Jimmy." The deputies didn't arrive at the scene until 3:33 p.m. The report stated that several individuals were standing around, including the camp's lawyer, Bruce Ellison; Russell Means; and a black man bearing the Indian name Wambli No Heart. Ellison told the officers that he had received a phone call at his office between 1:00 and 1:30 p.m. He advised them that they would find three empty shells in the gun belonging to the deceased, which was in the man's right hand. The report said the deceased was lying facedown on the ground with his head was pointing south. Post mortem lividity was present—that is to say, reddish splotches were visible where the blood had settled under the man's skin after death.

When the officers asked what had happened, all the men present, including Wambli No Heart, Smokey White Bull, and Evans White Face, told them an identical story. The sheriff's report recited their story as follows:

> They were out getting wood and were in the green camp truck. They were coming back and noticed the International Scout pickup camper belonging to the white man, and Wambli No Heart had gone to talk with the man, and then there were words, and the other two men, White Bull and White Face, came up. Their story was that the white man, Tollefson, pulled a gun on them, and

Wambli No Heart blocked it, and the gun went off. They stated that no one had seen the white man get hit with a bullet, and the three took off running, and they heard more shots as they ran.

Later that same afternoon, Wambli No Heart gave a taped statement to the sheriff's deputy Don Bahr. No Heart, a small, well-muscled, broad-shouldered, slim-hipped black man, wore his wiry hair in an Afro. His voice was masculine with a slight feminine undertone, which at certain words suggested a scolding woman. His face was thin and boyish, and he had a way of opening his large, pretty, bespectacled eyes very wide to emphasize what he was saying, giving himself an out-of-character innocence. The statement was as follows:

"Is Wambli your correct name?" the deputy asked.

"Yeah."

"And what happened?"

"Me and Evans and Smokey White Bull were fixin' to go out and pick up some wood. We left camp, maybe 'bout twelve, and we got the wood; took maybe forty-five minutes to an hour. And we come on to this vehicle parked on the ridge above our campsite."

"Near the flag?"

"Yes."

"Who was driving your truck?"

"Smokey. I was sitting on the passenger seat, and Evans was sitting in back, and I seen this male standing by the flag looking down on the campsite."

"He was just lookin' down?"

"Yeah. He looked to be in his late thirties or forties, somewhere around there. We stopped and asked this individual if he could come around down to the camp the correct way if he wanted to see the camp, because the people get nervous when they see people standing above on the ridge like that."

"What did he say?"

"Well, he proceeded back to his truck, and he seated himself behind the wheel, and from there on there was talk back and forth, and he said that if he wanted to see the camp, he didn't need to have our permission to look at it."

"Did he talk to you with his truck door open?"

"Yeah. He sat and talked with the door open."

"Wide open?"

"Yeah. Smokey was standing on my right and Evans on my left, and I was right in the middle."

"How long did you talk this way?"

"'Bout at least twenty minutes."

"And he never shut the door?"

"Not while I was standing there."

"What did you talk about?"

"Well, I said this was our home, that this is the Lakota's way of life, and he said, 'This is everybody's land,' and we went back and forth, and the voice I'm speaking in to you now is the voice I was speaking to him. I even used 'please.'"

"Did the man yell at you guys?"

"Only the last few—maybe ten—minutes. He was gettin' kinda bullshit and hysterical talkin' against us, you know, and that's when I felt a kind o' fear that, you know, that somethin' was fixin' to happen, because of the way he was talkin', and his eyes rollin' and . . ."

"Well, did you see any weapons?"

"I seen a pistol laying [*sic*] right on the passenger seat with the handle toward him, and a rifle was sittin' right there in front."

"And so, what happened?"

"Well, he started getting hysterical, you know, and all of a sudden my voice started going up a little bit, and I asked him, 'Man, would you please leave. There are kids and women here, and you got weapons in here,' and I seen the gun come up like this here, and I heard that shot fired, and then I heard one more shot."

"And what did you do?"

"Well, as soon as his hand came around, that's when I went like this here."

"What hand did you block him with?"

"This right here."

"With your left hand?"

"Yes."

"And so then you hit the gun?"

"I hit his forearm."

"So, you hit the gun and the hand before the gun went off?"

"Right."

"How was it pointed when it went off?"

"When it went off, I couldn't really tell you, because I'm telling you that's the first time I experienced something like that."

"What did you do then?"

"Well, if you'd seen that cliff—well, I don't think I could go down that cliff again—and as I ran down the cliff, I heard two more shots."

Wambli No Heart told the deputy that Russell Means got there before Bruce Ellison, and then Ellison and Means went back up on top of the ridge along with practically all the men in the camp—maybe fifteen or twenty were walking around up there, seeing what they could see. Wambli No Heart told Means what had happened, and then the officers had come. The camp had been having trouble—bikers harassing them and other people trying to make the camp look bad—but the Indian's reason for the camp was to do good, Wambli No Heart said.

"Is this the truth of what happened?" Deputy Bahr asked.

"It is the truth," No Heart said.

Wambli No Heart never mentioned the name of Collins Catch the Bear. His name never came up.

6.

By the time of Catch the Bear's murder trial in 1983, I'd been out of law school almost thirty years. I was fifty-four and had served as an elected prosecutor for two eight-year terms, I'd been trying cases around the country after the national spotlight was cast on me with my suit against the energy company Kerr-McGee for the plutonium poisoning of its whistleblower employee Karen Silkwood. (Silkwood's story became a celebrated movie starring Meryl Streep and Cher.) It was my memoir, *Gunning for Justice*, that had motivated Jim Leach to call me about helping him defend Collins Catch the Bear as first chair.

Six years before the killing of Clarence Tollefson, Leach had volunteered his services pro bono to the Wounded Knee Defense Committee, a group of lawyers dedicated to the defense of those charged with crimes arising from AIM's standoff in that desperate Indian hamlet on the Pine Ridge Indian Reservation known as Wounded Knee. A bouquet of criminal charges had been brought by the feds against many Indians involved in that standoff, including AIM leaders Russell Means and Dennis Banks. The charges against those two were eventually thrown out, and the government was itself found guilty of prosecutorial misconduct. A respected U.S. district judge, Fred Nichol, held that the government offered tainted testimony, sworn statements by witnesses that the prosecutor knew or should have known were false. The trial judge dismissed the case, concluding, "The fact that incidents of misconduct formed a pattern throughout the course of the trial leads me to the belief that this case was not prosecuted in good faith or in the spirit of justice. The waters of justice have been polluted, and dismissal, I believe, is the appropriate cure for the pollution in this case."

But that was then.

The news of Clarence Tollefson's killing on the ridge above the Yellow Thunder Camp hatched massive outrage among the local white citizenry. Both inside and outside Rapid City, one heard talk that sounded in substance like *Those fucking Indians killed another white man. They invaded the national forest. It's going to be Wounded Knee all over again.* The whites in Rapid City—and most of the city's residents were white—were angry, and afraid.

Jim Leach had followed the prosecutor's case against Collins Catch the Bear with mounting interest. For reasons he couldn't readily explain, he felt drawn to the case. At the time Leach entered the scene, Collins was being represented by a public defender who was staggering under the weight of an inhumane caseload—scores of cases, many hopeless—and was therefore delighted to have Leach substituted as Collins's lawyer. The two lawyers visited Collins in his jail cell, and Collins and Leach seemed to hit it off pretty well. Leach returned to Collins's cell a few days later, and Collins asked him to take his case. That's when Leach called me.

As I listened to this young lawyer explain the known facts of the case, I was touched by the notion of this kid just a few years out of law school worrying about another kid just a few years out of puberty. And Leach was worrying without a fee. Moved by Collins's story, I told Leach to bring all the materials he'd collected on the case to my place in Jackson Hole. I'd make no promises about joining him, but I'd at least go over the details of the case and share my thoughts with him.

Among other things, Leach told me that when the women at the Yellow Thunder Camp were told about Tollefson's shooting, they ran with the children and hid down in the canyon. If a white man was dead, other white men might come and kill everyone as they had at the 1864 Sand Creek Massacre, when the Colorado Militia attacked a peaceful Indian village, killing at least one hundred men, women, and children—even crawling babies. My great-grandfather had taken part in that infamous slaughter. Those who knew him said he never got over the guilt from it. He died at an early age. Perhaps this was my chance to cleanse the Spence blood of that ancient crime.

Within a few days, Leach arrived at my home in Jackson Hole along with his friend Carole. She was blonde with a trim, healthy look, like a PE major. She came off as timid, and deferred to Leach. He was lean, not as tall as me, and half as wide. He was close to handsome, with a boyish face and a well-trimmed black beard. He wore his straight, dark hair short like a respectable young businessman would. His small ears stuck out a little, and a slightly dished nose held a pair of dark-rimmed glasses that gave him a studious appearance.

Leach plunked down on my table a large cardboard box full of files, papers, and the sheriff's photos that had been furnished by the prosecutor in response to a court order. We sat out on the glassed-in sun porch looking through photos of blood and gore. I picked up one of the photos. Leach saw the repulsion on my face.

"There's blood in most of your murder cases, isn't there Mr. Spence?" He was smart. And polite.

The first photo showed Tollefson lying facedown behind the pickup camper he'd parked near the cliff's edge. His head was turned slightly to the right, and he'd bled out large quantities of blood, which surrounded his head like a crimson halo. His revolver was clutched in his right hand, as if in a death grip: a Ruger .357 with a two-inch barrel.

The dead man's finger was neatly curled around the trigger. The gun lay partially out of its leather holster. A gold-colored wristwatch with an expandable gold band had been pulled down into the open palm of his left hand. Both his hands were covered in blood, and blood had dripped down the length of his right forearm. The gun itself was free of blood.

For relief, I looked away from the grisly photos and into the clear, bright blue morning sky of late January Wyoming 1982. The air was thin and crisp, and distances seemed irrelevant here, as if one could reach out and stick one's thumb into the ribs of the universe. The Grand Tetons stood stark and still like sentries guarding the snow-covered valley below, and a lone cow moose nipped at the red willows a few hundred feet from the door. I thought the moose had the wisdom of innocence we had lost, the great knowledge of no-knowledge from which the moose had learned to live in harmony with nature.

"I'll tell you one thing," I said to Jim Leach, "one thing for sure. That .357 pistol was put in the man's hand *after* he was shot."

Leach said nothing.

"Look," I said, pointing to a picture of the bloody hand clutching the gun. "See how the blood suddenly stops when it reaches the gun? There's blood on his arms and hands, lots of it, but there's no blood on the gun." I was passing Leach the photos. "Something's not right here."

Leach was staring out at the cow moose.

"What do you say about that?" I prompted.

He shrugged his shoulders and kept staring out the window.

"What's more, who ever saw a man fall dead to the ground with the gun still clutched in his hand like that? When he fell, the gun would have been jarred out of his hand. It wouldn't be clutched in his hand with his finger still curled neatly around the trigger. As he died, both hands would have relaxed. See? The *left* hand is relaxed." I held up a photo. "But the right hand is clenched tightly around the gun. That gun was *put* in the dead man's hand *after* he died."

I had yet to discover that this young lawyer was quiet, thoughtful, and not prone to quick judgments, a trait that might have served me better.

I pressed on. "Look at the left hand. How do you suppose his watch got pulled down into his palm?"

"I don't know," Leach said.

"Of course you don't *know*. But if you're going to defend this case, you'll have to at least have a theory."

I waited. No response.

"A few things are pretty obvious to me," I continued. "Somebody pulled on that man by the left wrist, and whoever was pulling on him pulled his watch down into his palm. Here, let me show you." I demonstrated, pulling on Leach's left arm and moving his watch downward toward his palm.

"Could have happened that way," Leach conceded.

This kid had come all the way from South Dakota to get me interested in his case, and now that he was here, I couldn't get him to talk to me about it. I was aware that sometimes I scared people without realizing it. I changed the subject and quieted down, speaking as softly as I could.

"What was the path of the bullet?" I asked.

"It went in the back of the neck and came out his mouth, the pathologist's report says." Leach reached into his briefcase and handed me the report bearing the signature of the forensic pathologist, Dr. Bradley Randall of Sioux Falls. The report read:

At autopsy the principal finding was a single gunshot wound to the right posterior portion of the head. The bullet track extended slightly downward, forward, and to the transection of the right carotid artery. The gunshot wound produced death via hemorrhage from the transected carotid artery. The wound track extends downward and to the left passing through musculature at the base of the skull and then through the transverse processions of C2-3.

"So, what does this all mean?" I asked Leach.

He waited for me to give him my take on it.

I was looking at a photo that showed the entry wound. "It means this man was shot behind the right ear. The bullet had to go down, and I mean *down*, to get to the boney protrusions of the vertebrae—that's called 'the transverse process.' It means that the bullet traveled through his flesh and chipped away at the transverse processes of the second and third vertebrae of the neck. Right here." I pointed to the middle portion of the back of my own neck.

"I know," Leach said and smiled faintly, as if smiling were somehow against the rules.

I read aloud from the report: "'The bullet came out the base of the tongue and the left corner of the mouth.'"

I looked at the photo of Tollefson's face taken at the morgue, putting a magnifying glass to it. There was a small, irregular tear at the mouth that was said to be the exit wound. It was too small for any whole bullet, too small even for a .22. The tear was merely the wound made by a bullet fragment or from the edge of the whole bullet as it exited the mouth.

"The bullet came out through his open mouth," I said, looking carefully at the photo again.

Leach said nothing.

"And the weapon had to have been fired when Tollefson's head was well below the gun's muzzle."

Leach quietly said, "Yes, of course."

I glanced out at the cow moose, still grazing outside my window. "We're smarter than that moose out there," I said to Leach, "but not as wise, if that makes any sense."

"Yes," he said, as if he understood me for the first time. Then a mountain raven landed behind the moose in the snow. The raven began to waddle about, pecking where the moose had lately lain. "Raven eat moose dung in the winter," I said.

I turned to the sheriff's photos again. One was a close-up of the pickup camper's driver's seat, looking into the pickup through the open driver's-side door. There was no blood where the victim had been sitting. The inside of the driver's door was also barren of blood, which led to the conclusion that the door had been open when the man was shot.

On the ground on the driver's side where the driver would first step out of the cab, blood had dripped down, forming a ten-by-fourteen-inch pattern of spatter drops on the gravel. From the photos, it appeared that Tollefson had been grabbed by the left wrist and pulled around so that when he was shot, although he was still seated in the cab, his feet were on the ground and his head was extended out of the cab. Also, in the act of pulling Tollefson by the wrist, someone had pulled the victim's watch down into his palm.

The pathologist had cut through the neck muscles to expose the course of the bullet. The bullet must have expanded as it passed though the neck, gouging out a hole the size of my index finger before exiting Tollefson's open mouth and smashing into the side of his pickup camper, creating a hole about three-quarters of an inch in diameter. Blood must have spurted out the entry wound, depositing widespread blood spatter on the ground below where Tollefson had been sitting when he was shot.

Inside the pickup cab, mounted on a rack on top of the dash, was a .22-250 rifle equipped with a high-powered scope. On the floor behind the gearshift lever was a large ammunition box marked ".22-250."

A sheriff's photo showed two stickers on the rear bumper of Tollefson's pickup. One read, "The West Wasn't Won with a Registered Gun." The other read, "When Guns Are Outlawed, Only Outlaws Will Have Guns."

"You could blow the head off a sparrow at two hundred yards with that .22-250 rifle," I said to Leach.

He nodded.

"It's a sniper rifle," I continued. "Fast, powerful, low trajectory."

"Target rifle," Leach said. "Targets are behind the seat. Look here." He handed me a photo.

"Yeah. Camouflage jacket and pants behind the seat, too," I said, pointing.

"State will claim he was a turkey hunter," Leach said.

"July twenty-first isn't turkey season in South Dakota." I paused. "What do you know about this Tollefson fellow anyway?"

"Nothing much," Leach said. "He lived on the edge of Rapid City. Retired enlisted man out of the service, air force. About forty-nine. There's two moose over there!" Leach said abruptly, pointing. Another moose, larger than the first, had come out from behind a high, thick willow bush to nip at the shoots. "Prehistoric-looking beasts," he said.

"Yeah," I replied. "The bigger one is a bull. He's shed his horns already. He'll grow a new set in the spring." I turned back to the photos. "What else do you know about Tollefson?"

"Don't know much more," Leach said.

"Maybe he was undercover for the government."

Leach didn't answer.

I couldn't connect with this kid. I knew he cared about Catch the Bear. After all, he had come to see me in Wyoming at his own expense, likely out of his meager savings.

"What do you call that thing hanging down under that big moose's chin?" Leach asked.

"A waddle," I said. "So, got any theories about the federal marshals, maybe the FBI?"

"No," Leach said.

"What the hell was Tollefson doing up there?"

"Maybe the state will say he was a photographer," Leach said. "Belonged to a photography club in Rapid."

"He didn't have a camera with him. All he had was a sniper's rifle, a snub-barreled .357, and a lot of ammunition. You don't shoot turkeys with a snub-barreled .357 revolver. You'd agree with that, wouldn't you?"

"Well, yes," Leach said in an almost plaintive voice. Then he gave me a smile as if everything was all right between us and always had been. I smiled back.

A series of photographs had been taken along the driver's side of the pickup body from the open door to the rear of the camper, where the body had been found. Tollefson, leaning against the camper body, had staggered down its length, leaving a trail of blood on the camper's body. When he reached the camper's end, he took one last step that crossed the line into eternity. He'd then fallen facedown to the ground, dead.

The blood beneath Tollefson separated that small piece of earth from the rest of the world. There in the gravel, life and death had passed each other without even a friendly nod. There, Tollefson's blood enriched the earth, and I thought the earth blessed him back. I thought it a good place for any man to die, and that Clarence Tollefson, who, they said, was an outdoorsman, would have thought so, too.

7.

On August 9, 1982, Rodney Lefholz, the prosecutor, called a grand jury. He'd given Samuel J. C. Lone Wolf, age thirty-two, total immunity for his testimony, meaning that if Lone Wolf were involved in any criminal act related to Tollefson's death, he would not be prosecuted for it. We had the transcript of Lone Wolf's testimony to the grand jury. He had a lot to say under oath.

Lone Wolf, a college graduate and ex-marine, claimed that he'd been working with AIM at its office in Rapid City when Russell Means phoned him and instructed him to leave work and get to the Yellow Thunder Camp immediately. Lone Wolf was driven to the camp by an Indian he called Shorty, who told him that a white man had been killed. When Lone Wolf got to the camp, he was met by Means. Some other Indians were hanging around and joking about who was going to get the dead man's pickup camper.

During the grand jury proceedings, a juror asked Lone Wolf why he had come forward with his testimony. Lone Wolf answered: "The way I grew up and my religious beliefs—that night [following the shooting of Tollefson] I did a lot of thinking. What was going on does not go with my religious beliefs and my way of being—I don't deal with lies. I am not going to cover up for anybody, and I knew I did wrong by wiping the fingerprints off [the door handle of Tollefson's camper], and that whole night it just kind of ate me up, and I couldn't deal with it, and I am a pretty strong person spiritually. I had to come out and speak the truth. I felt an injustice was done, and it had to be corrected."

Under questioning by Prosecutor Lefholz, Lone Wolf told the grand jury something that was not only startling, but that put law enforcement on notice that when they later charged Collins Catch the Bear with murder, they were charging the wrong person.

Lone Wolf described the scene to the grand jury. He said that he saw the .357 Magnum firmly in the dead man's hand, the gun partially out of its holster. Both the driver's and passenger's doors of the pickup were open, the passenger-side door open only four or five inches. He told how the blood was evident along the driver's side of the camper, and he described the large bullet hole in the side of the pickup. Lone Wolf said he thought the scene "stunk," that it didn't look right. He said he'd spent time in Vietnam, "and the angle of the bullet entry in the neck didn't look like an accident to me."

Under questioning from Lefholz, Lone Wolf told the grand jury that Wambli No Heart said he'd argued with the guy in the camper, and the guy had pulled a gun on him. At first No Heart said that he'd grabbed Tollefson. Then Lone Wolf said Heart changed his statement and said that he'd "blocked the gun" when Tollefson pulled it on him.

"No Heart was relating this to Russell Means?" Lefholz asked Lone Wolf.

"That's correct. I was right there with Russell. Skip was there, Smokey, the chubby guy, Catch the Bear, China, Drifter, Tom Gammon, Mike, and American Horse were all there by that time."

Lefholz asked Lone Wolf, "What happened after No Heart described this blocking motion?"

"Russell said to Skip and the chubby guy not to worry about anything, that they would not be involved. He sent me down to get a camera and to tell the people to make sure the camp was clean," he said, meaning that all their weapons were fully hidden. "Then Means told Janice from Idaho and Shorty Black Smith to go back to town and get the camp's attorneys, Bruce Ellison and Jan Hamil." Lone Wolf said that Means picked Smokey White Bull, Evans White Face, and No Heart as the people who would come forward to be interrogated by the police. Lone Wolf said, "The persons who actually saw everything happen were Skip; the chubby guy, an Indian approximately 210, 230 pounds and about five ten; and Wambli No Heart."

"So, Russell substituted Smokey and Evans for Skip and the chubby guy?"

"Yes."

Lone Wolf recounted how Means had argued that Skip was a family man, and according to Indian tradition, family men do not come forward. They should be kept safe, "out of the scene." Lone Wolf said Means did not trust the chubby guy, because he hadn't been at the camp that long, and Means felt he might break. Smokey had been in jail, as had Wambli No Heart and Evans, and Means thought those three could therefore stand the pressure of interrogation. Means's order to substitute witnesses who had *not* been present at the shooting for those who *had* been present was heard by at least a dozen persons gathered there that day, including Collins Catch the Bear.

According to Lone Wolf, Bruce Ellison arrived about fifteen or twenty minutes later. He walked up to the ridge and asked what had happened. Lone Wolf testified to the grand jury that Means told Ellison that "the white man was here overlooking the ridge, and he got in an argument with No Heart and the white man pulled his gun out, and No Heart blocked the gun, and a round went off. No Heart said they took off running down the hill. Then they later came back and checked the body when a couple more rounds went off."

A couple more rounds went off after the killing? This strange assertion was never again made by any witness or anyone else.

I wondered if Means knew that there were three spent cartridges in the cylinder of the .357. Was that why some of the witnesses were claiming they'd heard other shots? For someone to have discovered that the pistol's cylinder contained three spent cartridges, that person would have had to take the gun in his hands, release the cylinder, observe the empty cartridge cases, and then put the gun back into the dead man's hand.

Lone Wolf said that Wambli No Heart was not the black man's real name. His true name was James Lee Jones Jr. Lone Wolf didn't like the man. Here's Lone Wolf's description of Wambli No Heart:

"Wambli is approximately five seven, five eight, about 160 pounds, medium built, very wide shoulders for his height, a black man, very cynical, nasty type attitude, that 'I am the boss, and either you listen to me or get the hell out.' He was responsible for security of the camp even though at the time this whole incident happened he was on the verge of getting kicked out."

Wambli told Lone Wolf that he'd done "flat time," which meant he'd served his full sentence; he said he'd killed a man in prison.

Lone Wolf told the grand jury that he asked No Heart if he'd touched the Tollefsen vehicle.

"Yes, I opened the doors," No Heart admitted.

"That's stupid," Lone Wolf said he told No Heart. "You don't open doors."

I continued to read Lone Wolf's grand jury testimony: "Then Russell Means looked at me and said, 'Wipe the fingerprints off,' and I took the chubby guy's shirt, which he had off, and wiped the door handles."

"With reference to the body, was it moved or altered?" Lefholz asked Lone Wolf.

Lone Wolf's answer: "The only thing I can think of was the holster being put back on the gun. *The gun was holstered before we got back*" (my emphasis).

The sheriff's photos showed the pistol in Tollefson's hand but partially out of its holster. Was Lone Wolf saying that when he first came upon the scene, and before he'd gone down to tell the people to clean up the camp [i.e., hide all firearms], the dead man's pistol had been *out of its holster* and was put back into its holster while Lone Wolf was gone?

Lefholz didn't ask any more questions to explain Lone Wolf's answer.

One thing I remembered: The FBI made no finding of gunshot residue inside the holster.

"Did Wambli No Heart ever say he was inside the vehicle?" Lefholz asked Lone Wolf.

Lone Wolf's answer: "Yes. He said that when he grabbed the man's wrist that he opened the door from the *passenger side, that he had gone in* (my emphasis) and tried to talk to the man, calm him down supposedly, and that's when the man pulled the gun out, he grabbed his wrist, and then he said he blocked it."

Lefholz asked: "And Wambli No Heart would be in the *passenger side* [my emphasis] of the pickup?"

Lone Wolf: "That's correct."

Lone Wolf went on to say that No Heart was standing next to Russell Means and "indicated to Means that No Heart grabbed the man with his left hand first and then with his right, and when No Heart grabbed the man[,] the gun went off. He indicated to Russ [that] he grabbed Tollefson's right arm from where they *were standing at*" (again my emphasis).

Lefholz: "And then he switched it to 'blocked the gun'?"

Lone Wolf: "Yes. Then he changed his statement and said, 'No, I blocked it.' From what I [saw when I] looked at the bullet wound and the blood coagulated in the back of the man's neck, the way he was laying [*sic*] and everything, I knew there was no possible way that he [Wambli No Heart] could have blocked it. The only way that something like that could have happened, and knowing Wambli personally, knowing his strength—that it had to be that he grabbed the man's wrist and that the gun went off."

Or, I thought, one might as easily surmise that No Heart simply grabbed the gun from Tollefson and shot him with it.

The bullet's course was steeply down from the base of the skull into the boney processes of the first and second vertebrae, in the neck, and out the corner of the mouth. To account for the steep downward angle of the bullet's course, Tollefson would have to have been holding the pistol in his right hand with his elbow almost pointing to the sky, or he would somehow have to have been pushed down in the seat with Wambli's hand holding the gun above him when the trigger was pulled. In other words, there had to have been a wrestling match of some kind going on inside the cab of that vehicle.

There was a piece of cardboard behind the front seats. Lone Wolf described a hole the size of a .357 Magnum bullet through the cardboard: "A .357 makes a regular entry hole, but the exit through bone and flesh of that type of bullet makes a pretty big hole." Lone Wolf thought the cardboard was hit after the bullet had gone through Tollefson. "The cardboard was right back here (pointing to the back area behind the seat). There was blood on the side of the hole." That was the last we ever heard of that piece of cardboard from any other witness or anyone else. Lone Wolf finally concluded that the gun was not in Tollefson's hand when he was shot.

We had those sheriff's photos showing Tollefson's hand firmly gripping the .357 as he lay dead on the ground. For the dead man's fingers still to be wrapped tightly around the pistol grip as he lay face-down, he would have to have been holding on to the pistol with a strong grip *after* he was shot and while he staggered out of the camper on the driver's side.

One could see where he had then stumbled to the ground, regained his feet, and then struggled along the camper's body, leaving his bloody trail on it. He therefore would *still* have to have been holding the pistol firmly when he reached the rear of the camper, where he bled out before falling to the ground dead, face-down—the pistol gripped tightly in his hand, as shown in the photos.

And we remember, his right hand was completely covered with blood, but not a drop of blood was on the pistol. Someone had put the pistol in the man's hand *after* he was dead.

Did Tollefson shoot at his assailant twice more as he staggered out the pickup's driver-side door? We remember that after the first shot, everyone supposedly ran down the hill. But Lone Wolf quoted Means as claiming that those who'd been present at the time of the shooting later came back to check the body *when a couple more rounds went off* (my emphasis)."

Who would have fired twice more, and why? There had to have been three shots to account for the three empty cartridges in the gun. Somebody had forgotten his lines.

Lefholz then asked Lone Wolf, "Did Bruce [Ellison] have any objections to switching the individuals?" But where in the record was any testimony that Ellison knew that Means had switched the witnesses? Was Lefholz trying to elicit damaging testimony against Ellison by leading his witness with facts not uttered from the lips of any witness?

"No, he did not object," Lone Wolf answered. "Bruce pretty much understands Indians by being around the camp and being indoctrinated. He understands them very much."

Yes, I thought, Ellison knew his Indian clients. But I had no reason then and I have no reason now to believe that Bruce Ellison ever knowingly testified to a falsehood under oath or took part in any alleged crime such as suborning perjury.

Was Lefholz again attempting to incriminate Ellison when he

asked, "Did you say Bruce took the people aside to coach them on their story?"

"Yes, he did," Lone Wolf replied.

As every lawyer appreciates, reviewing a witness's testimony with him before he takes the stand is one thing. Teaching a witness falsehoods and asking him to testify to such falsehoods is the crime of suborning perjury. If the latter were proven in a court of law against Ellison, he could lose his license and, if convicted, be sent to the pen.

I knew Ellison's reputation. He was a hard-fighting cause lawyer, but no one to my knowledge had ever suggested—nor do I—that he stepped over the line. And Lefholz never sought an indictment against either Russell Means or Bruce Ellison.

Lefholz had kept his impaneling of this grand jury secret until the subpoenas had been issued and placed in the hands of the sheriff for service. Then he let the media know, and that immediately lifted the candidate for state's attorney general into statewide stories. On August 5, 1982, the *Rapid City Journal* reported:

> Pennington County State's Attorney, Rod Lefholz, announced the grand jury investigation of the shooting death of Clarence Tollefson Wednesday afternoon as deputy sheriffs were on their way to the camp in several squad cars to serve subpoenas on witnesses.

Bruce Ellison claimed the grand jury was "a politically-motivated fishing expedition because Lefholz is running for attorney general and the Sheriff, Mel Larson, is also running for re-election."

Thirty-six subpoenas had been issued, and many who'd been served followed the example of their leader, Russell Means, and refused to testify. Means issued a prepared statement challenging "the legitimacy of the grand jury which has been called for the purpose of racist persecution and political expediency." He said that for a tribal member to testify would only serve the political ambitions of the prosecuting attorney, Rodney Lefholz, who wanted to be elected attorney general, and of the sheriff, who wanted to be reelected.

Nicholas Meinhardt, a white member of the Yellow Thunder Camp and director of the Rapid City office of the Quakers, the American Friends Service Committee, said the decision to testify or not was an individual one for each camp member, but he said he would refuse to testify on the grounds that he was "a guest within the boundaries of the Lakota Nation as guaranteed by the 1868 Ft. Laramie Treaty," and that the court therefore had no jurisdiction over him.

None of this seemed to deter Rodney Lefholz. He calmly replied in the press that he didn't anticipate having to go through contempt proceedings with any of the witnesses, although he was prepared to do so if necessary. "Anyone who's not afraid of the truth shouldn't be afraid of the grand jury," he said.

The next day, Russell Means charged that Clarence Tollefson had appeared above the camp a year before and had been taking pictures, and even then, Means said, they'd invited him to come down and visit the camp in a proper manner, but that Tollefson had replied, "I don't give a damn what you want." Then he drew a .45 automatic pistol, cocked it, and drove off. Somebody in the camp got Tollefson's license plate number.

On August 17, 1981, almost a year before the shooting, Bruce Ellison sent Sheriff Mel Larson a letter describing this incident. He gave the sheriff the license plate number and requested an investigation. The sheriff didn't respond.

Means charged that Tollefson had tried to get into the rear of the camp on two prior occasions. He didn't go into detail, but he claimed that Sheriff Larson had failed to investigate any of the camp's complaints of threatened violence. He cited prior incidents involving shots being fired in the vicinity of the camp and guns in the hands of hostile whites who'd threatened two of the camp's women. Means demanded the resignation of Sheriff Mel Larson, arguing that if this had been a peaceful white camp, and if Indians had been pulling guns and threatening the whites, there sure as hell would have been an investigation. It sounded like the white and Indian wars were about to be reignited.

Lefholz said he was prepared to start contempt proceedings against any member of the camp who refused to cooperate with his grand jury probe. "Nobody is going to thumb their nose at the grand jury," he warned.

It was about this time that Jim Leach, a friend of Bruce Ellison, first got involved in the Tollefson case. Ellison had asked Leach to represent him when Ellison was called to testify before the grand jury. Lone Wolf had already testified, but before any other witness was called, Lefholz suddenly dismissed all the subpoenas and announced that the grand jury would not meet that week as scheduled. He said he wasn't at liberty to discuss the matter further.

But Russell Means was prepared to discuss it. He told the press, "I believe Lefholz has begun to realize the futility of this witch hunt. He's going to prolong this as long as he can in order to further his political campaign."

Then, on September 27, 1982, Rodney Lefholz dismissed the grand jury. His reason wasn't revealed until it was learned that Wambli No Heart had changed his story. No Heart now claimed that Clarence Tollefson was shot in the back of the head with a .22 rifle by Collins Catch the Bear.

By Collins Catch the Bear?

With a .22 rifle?

Collins was hauled before the court in Rapid City on "an information" filed against him by Lefholz. An information is a formal criminal charge made by a prosecutor without the necessity of obtaining a grand jury indictment. A preliminary hearing follows the information to determine what the law calls "probable cause," that is, do the known facts support a probability that the person charged is guilty of the crime? As American citizens, we are not to be tried for a crime unless there is *probable cause* that we committed it.

Jim Leach told me that when the court appointed the public defender in Rapid City to represent Collins, Collins pled "not guilty," but the magistrate, Roland Grosshans, who was also the circuit judge, found there was sufficient cause presented at the preliminary hearing to bind Collins over for trial on a charge of murder in the first degree, and he ordered Collins held without bond in the Pennington County Jail pending trial.

Leach said, "Along the way the public defender and Lefholz made a deal to plead Collins guilty. Lefholz and the public defender went into the judge's chambers together, like friends, and closed the door behind them. Collins wasn't there, of course. He was still sweating it out in jail." I saw it all in the transcript of the court record.

"Your Honor," the public defender said. "Sir, we have come to an agreement on Catch the Bear." Whether Collins had agreed to this agreement is not clear. "He will be willing to plead guilty to first-degree manslaughter, and the state agrees to a sentence of no more than thirty years."

Judge Roland Grosshans was a big man, still hanging on to the edge of youth. He had pure white hair but a handsome, boyish face that came off as a bit older because of a heavy black mustache that covered his full upper lip. His dark, roguish eyes spoke before he spoke, and he wore glasses. Folks thought he looked like a judge should look.

Judge Grosshans said, "Thirty years, huh?" He had a rich, good-to-listen-to voice.

"Yes, Your Honor, sir," Lefholz agreed.

"Well, well," Judge Grosshans said. "What do we need a judge for, then? You gentlemen have it all worked out."

"Yes, sir," the public defender said.

"Well, Mr. Public Defender, you may plead the defendant guilty if you like, but I can give you no assurance that the sentence won't be more than thirty years. This killing is a very serious matter."

"Yes, Your Honor," the public defender said.

"Is there any further business before the court?" the judge inquired.

"Well, sir, you couldn't accept our agreement?" the public defender asked.

"I can't tell you whether I would or wouldn't sentence Catch the Bear to thirty years or less. Depends on the facts. I'd have to hear the facts. But I won't agree to such a sentence beforehand. We're not buying and selling a used car here. First-degree manslaughter can carry life, as you gentlemen know. Punishment, gentlemen, is not a matter of a bargain, like some market commodity. Punishment is a matter of justice, gentlemen."

"Yes, sir," the public defender said, and that was all the record revealed of the matter.

I believed Lefholz was prosecuting the wrong man. Like the rest of us, prosecutors can and do make mistakes. The cynical might argue that Lefholz was running for attorney general in South Dakota and was seeking the publicity that the conviction of Tollefson's killer would afford. Collins Catch the Bear was an easy mark. But the annals of American jurisprudence bulge with stories of the innocent who've been mistakenly convicted, almost always the poor and powerless.

I knew that in the eyes of the state's white power structure, Collins was just another one of those AIM Indians, a member of that Russell Means gang at that illegitimate Yellow Thunder Camp.

Sitting on the sunporch at my Wyoming home with Jim Leach in late January 1982, looking over the crime scene photos, I asked him, "Why get involved in a murder case like this? The responsibility is like a blind surgeon operating as best he can on a patient in terminal agony. We'll have jurors deciding the case, people we don't know. Some hide their prejudices and are dangerous. The prosecutor will play games with us and hold back evidence and witnesses. As a lawyer, I can never know how I come off to jurors. Some may distrust me. Some may despise me, and I'll never know it. The judge is a politician and has to stand for reelection. He has an interest in the outcome of the case. A conviction of Collins will likely help him. If I make a mistake in a murder trial, it's like that blind surgeon who cuts something he shouldn't and the patient dies: the risks are too high. Everybody's at risk in the trial of a murder case."

Leach was mute, waiting for what was yet to come.

I argued on: "If I lose the case when I should have won, I could never get over it."

Leach nodded his understanding. Then he said, "That's why I'm here asking for your help."

"So, why did *you* get involved?" I asked.

"I don't know," Leach replied, seeming his distant self again. Then he added, "I just thought it was the right thing to do." His face showed pain. Then he gazed out at the cow moose again, still nipping at the winter willows.

The raven had flown.

8.

The prosecuting attorney, Rodney Lefholz, was asking for the death penalty against Collins.

Death.

"Even if he's guilty, this isn't a death penalty case," Jim Leach said. He could sound like an attorney, all right. "None of the required aggravating circumstances is present, like killing a cop or killing in the commission of a robbery, or something like that. Everybody knows this isn't a death penalty case."

I said, "No, Jim. Lefholz will claim Catch the Bear killed out of hatred for whites, that he intended to kill Tollefson, premeditated the killing, and that this is a clear case of first-degree murder, which carries the death penalty."

Yeah, I suppose," Leach finally admitted. "Before I got into the case, Collins had been sitting in that damned iron-and-concrete hole for three months with that death penalty charge hanging over him. Nobody can tell you how it is to be trapped in a stinking cell like that at twenty, or any age, helplessly waiting for white men who hate you to decide whether you live or die." He continued:

"In my opinion, Lefholz wanted to sweat a plea out of Collins—wring it out of his guts."

"Sweat a plea and save a trial," I said.

"Collins has incredible strength," Leach said. "Collins is very brave. They never let him out to exercise once for those three months. He never saw the sun—stuck in that one cell night and day with the death penalty hanging over him. And he maintained his innocence through all that."

Leach saw the horror on my face.

"Put yourself in the position Collins was in," he continued. "An Indian caught up in the white man's justice system. Suppose you, a white man, are arrested on the reservation and locked up in some foul Indian jail. Suppose you're defended by an Indian public defender on the tribal payroll, and you're held in that damned Indian jail three months—no exercise, poor food—and you're going to be tried by an all-Indian jury for killing an Indian. And an Indian judge is going to sit on your case, and the Indian prosecutor wants to kill you and is asking for the death penalty, and your appointed Indian attorney is doing nothing for you. He has too many other cases to work on. He knows that no matter what he does, you're going to die anyway. What would you do if they offered you thirty years for a guilty plea and you could save your life? Would you take it?" Leach asked.

I didn't answer. I couldn't go there.

9.

Rodney Lefholz was tall, probably six foot three, a man past thirty. The day I met him, he was wearing a blue suit, slightly mussed. At a distance, he displayed a tough-looking face, like that of a veteran boxer, with pugilistic shadows around the eyes and a nose that might once have been broken. Up close, he appeared less aggressive. A clump of freshly washed dark hair hung down over the tops of his ears, giving him an open, relaxed, masculine, even handsome appearance. He spoke in a plain, disarming voice and wore a slightly crooked smile.

His voice and demeanor were of a thoroughly nice guy whom everybody ought to love, a guy who said "gosh" and "golly" a lot, in the way of an appealing South Dakota farm boy just trying to do right—and who wanted to be the state's new attorney general. Roland Grosshans, the circuit judge, had encouraged the young Lefholz to run for the job. Although they were of opposite political faiths, the judge said he thought Rodney would be a good attorney general, and Lord knows, the state needed good men in office.

Lefholz entered the attorney general race calling himself a tough prosecutor with a 100 percent conviction rate in drug and homicide cases and a 92 percent rate in drunk driving cases. He said, "I've built this record with nothing more than just good old-fashioned hard work." He said, "I won't let campaigning affect my job as state's attorney. I was elected for the job—a twenty-four-hours-a-day, seven-days-a-week job."

Rodney Lefholz was a Democrat, and in a predominantly Republican state, he needed all the help he could muster in his run for South Dakota's attorney general. Then, on July 21, 1982, Clarence Tollefson was killed, and it was as if fate were smiling on Lefholz. He'd been handed the case of an Indian charged with killing a white man at Yellow Thunder Camp, an AIM invasion on the National Forest. The case was a ready-made war cry for Lefholz's campaign.

Lefholz was doubtlessly aware of one simple rule of politics in South Dakota: attack AIM. After all, demonizing AIM had been a sure way to the governor's mansion for William Janklow, who was carried into office on the public's outcry over the white and Indian hostilities at Wounded Knee. Governor Janklow was quoted as saying, "The only way to deal with the Indian is to put a gun to the AIM leader's head and pull the trigger."

An overwhelming majority of South Dakota voters despised the American Indian Movement. Smoldering at the core of many white people of South Dakota was a history of hostility and violence. The ranchers still drove their pickup trucks with a .30-30 carbine across the back window, and many hadn't forgotten what the Sioux had done to Custer. The poisonous epitaph of the Old West hung on: "The only good injun is a dead injun."

The 1868 Treaty of Fort Laramie had plainly and simply awarded the Black Hills to the Lakota Sioux, "for as long as the grass shall grow and the rivers flow." But then, only a few years following the signing of the treaty, gold was discovered in the Black Hills, "the yellow-metal-that-makes-white-man crazy," and the Paha Sapa was invaded by hordes of whites under the protection the U.S. government.

It wasn't until 1980 that the U.S. Supreme Court found that the United States had violated its treaty with the Sioux and had taken back the Black Hills illegally. But even then, the Court didn't return the land to the Indians. Instead, it awarded them only white man's money—$122 million, which amounted to something like the price of an old, about-to-fall-apart used car for each of the sixty thousand eligible Indians.

AIM resisted the theft. "It's pocket change for our sacred land," Means said. And no one would dispute that it was a cheap price for what could be one of the most valuable pieces of real estate on the continent.

I wondered if Clarence Tollefson, a professed outdoorsman, might not have sat down with Russell Means and Bruce Ellison under the great pines of the Paha Sapa and gazed with them into the quiet waters of Victoria Lake. Perhaps they would have agreed that the multinational corporations of America that threatened to destroy the Black Hills with their mining and timbering and pollution ought to be chased out by a confederation of white men and red men, so that those holy hills could be preserved for all mankind. Perhaps they could have smoked the pipe and sent their prayers to Wakan Tanka, the same god as the white man's god. Perhaps the power of their combined prayers could have saved this place from corporate invaders whose agenda was to transform these pristine lands into dead money.

Bruce Ellison said, "Because of economic interests, the government is pitting the red man and white man against each other. Whites are opposed to corporations coming in here, and so are Indians, so the government is employing a kind of divide-and-conquer approach. They are trying to knock out the opposition with a tactical diversion: their attack on the Yellow Thunder Camp."

Russell Means agreed. "The enemy of the Indian is not his

white brother," he said. "The enemy is the multinational corporation, which is the enemy of all mankind."

I thought a cruel irony had come to pass. The white American male is, by his genes, also a hunter, and having once driven the Indian from his sacred hunting grounds, the white man now feels the desperation of also being driven from the land. He hears the crying out of his cells, and he feels invaded, conquered by whom or what he does not understand.

"The people are told they are free," I said to Leach.

"Yes?" He sat down with an air of patience, preparing himself for one of my sermons.

"We are all the victims of a powerful propaganda machine. Our parents, our teachers, and our history books tell us we're free. We hear that over and over on television. But our masters are the multinational corporations, who, we are told, are just a blissful conglomerate of caring people. Even our Supreme Court has given the nonliving corporation, that physically is nothing more than a piece of paper filed somewhere, the same rights as a living person."

"It's crazy," Leach said.

"Now the white man, perhaps the likes of Tollefson, has been told by his corporate overlord that the Indians at Yellow Thunder Camp are the thieves. And the white man believes the corporate propaganda machine and does not understand that the corporate conglomerate owns even his ears."

In those days, the white majority in South Dakota liked to separate Indians into two kinds: good Indians and bad. Most were said to be bad. The good Indians were referred to with lingering scorn as "apples"—they were "red on the outside and white on the inside." These were the surrendered Indians, the ones who groveled at the feet of their white masters. Apple Indians were nothing new in South Dakota politics. As early as Crazy Horse, some chose not to fight for the Indians' holy land and life. Some appeased the whites and joined them in their easier ways. The Indians used to call this kind of Indian the "Hangs-around-the-fort."

"My grandfather laid down his rifle at Fort Laramie in 1868," Roger White told me. White's name had been White Face, but he waited until his father died before he applied to the court for the name change. "The Indian Wars have been over for a hundred years," he said. "My family has tried hard to better itself. My father got little schooling on the reservation. No minority can advance without education. The Bureau of Indian Affairs established boarding schools. We kids left home to go to school. It was hard on us to leave our parents.

"Other Indians refused to send their kids to school," White said. "They were mostly drunks and ne'er-do-wells whose families had never settled down, and their kids are drunks, and are part of that terrorist organization, AIM, which gives the Indian a black eye. AIM gathers up all the malcontents on the reservation, and they attack the whites and cry about broken treaties and all the rest. For me, AIM is a laugh. The wars are over. It's time to get on with our lives and try to make something of ourselves and something for our kids."

When the sheriff's deputy found Tollefson's body sprawled in the bloody gravel behind his pickup camper, the first persons he wanted to talk to were, of course, Russell Means and Bruce Ellison. Means told the deputy he had nothing to say. But Ellison thought maybe the matter could be cleared up right away without a lot of fuss—before things got out of hand and more vigilantes attacked and before an unfortunate homicide disintegrated into another full-blown white and Indian war.

Ellison said he would talk to the sheriff and try to put things to rest so that the camp's fragile position in court wasn't damaged. He knew the government would exploit the killing of a white man in its campaign to close the camp. So, Ellison made a visit to the Sheriff's Office.

He was wearing a short-sleeved shirt and a pair of jeans. His hair, as always, was in a single long braid down the back that swayed as he walked. About thirty-two, with a good face and a quick smile, Ellison seemed a decent enough fellow, people said. But for the pigtail, he'd be a man you could trust right off.

Jim and I had been at the Sheriff's Office in Rapid City gathering some information the court had ordered, and we got to talking about Ellison with the deputy we were working with.

"Ya can't trust no sombitch who wears his hair in a goddamned pigtail," the deputy said. "Tries to look like an Injun, and he ain't an Injun. He mus' be only half Injun—only got one braid." He laughed at his own joke. "All I can tell ya is there's somethin' a little strange about a guy who wears his hair in a goddamned pigtail. And he's a lawyer, too. But then ya can't never tell what a lawyer'll do." He gave us that look and laughed again.

Bruce Ellison had walked right into the sheriff's interview room, and he didn't have to wait, because Deputy Don Bahr was ready for him. A tape recorder sat on the table. (By court order, the sheriff provided us with a copy of the interview.) Bahr motioned to Ellison to take a seat.

"We want to get this thing cleared up as soon as possible," Ellison said.

"When did you first become aware of any happenings at the camp?" Bahr asked.

"A fellow who works at the Alliance Office told me there was a shooting at the camp—I remember seeing a digital clock on the First Bank of South Dakota on the corner of Seventh and St. Joe, which said about two o'clock. I went out to the camp."

"When you got there, what'd ya see?"

"I saw Russ Means and some other people there. I went up on the ridge to see what happened. I saw the dead man—his eyes appeared slightly open—there was no breathing. There were flies around him already. The first thing I asked was if anybody had called law enforcement, and since no one had, I suggested that law enforcement be contacted immediately. Somebody called down—think it was Russ who called down to the camp."

Ellison went on with his statement without prompting. "We waited for the sheriff's department, and in the meantime, I tried to find out what [had] happened. I'm quite familiar with the repeated incidents of people going up there [on the ridge] and shouting obscenities, throwing rocks, throwing bottles down on people, and there's been a lot of threats against the camp. It seems that Wambli No Heart, the black fellow, went over and tried to talk to the white man, that [Tollefson] got back in his vehicle and the discussion continued, and the other people joined Wambli, and at some point, after fifteen or twenty minutes, Wambli, who had seen a pistol on the seat—"

Ellison stopped and thought for a moment. "One of the things I don't think I told you—I can't remember whether it was Smokey or Wambli. But one of the two gentlemen had mentioned—might have been Wambli—that as soon as the man got in his vehicle, the first thing he did was pick up a box of .22-250 shells and threw it up on the dashboard. And I remember after this I walked over to the vehicle. I saw a box of .22-250 shells down near the stick shift."

"Okay," the deputy said.

"I talked to the people there. I asked, 'Did anybody touch anything?' And the response I got was 'No.' Everybody said, 'No, that it was best if things were left right there where they were, that the evidence would speak for itself, and everybody was in agreement that they wanted to get this matter cleared up as quickly as possible, because no matter what happened, it would be bad for the camp."

"So, in other words, you heard comments and got information from Smokey, No Heart, and Evans White Face?"

"I didn't really talk to Evans," Ellison said.

"Were the stories pretty consistent? Did you feel there was any staging of it—ah, do you feel it happened just the way they said?"

"I saw nothing, nor did I hear anything that would lead me to believe anything different. Some of the people wanted to look into the truck, but I said, 'Stay away,' and the people told me no one had touched anything."

"Were you aware of where he was hit?"

"No. Wambli said he knocked the gun up, and everybody said Wambli just blocked it up, and they heard a shot, and the impression I got was that no one was even aware that the man had been hit until later—because it was pretty much a block and run—because when the first shot went off, people didn't stick around to find out what was going on.

"The people at the camp heard the shooting. There was concern that the man was still alive—that he might start shooting down at the camp—and the women and children moved to a back area, and in the meantime, Drifter came down and reported the man was lying down, and he checked him, and he was dead, and that's when Russ and the other people came up to see what [had] happened."

"Did you talk to Russ Means about it?"

"Just very briefly. He was in town when this thing happened."

"Okay," Deputy Bahr said. "Is there anything else at this time, Bruce, that you can think of?"

"I was surprised that the man's gun was in his holster."

"Why do you say that?"

"Well, just because it's not the normal thing that somebody's going to do—to shoot through their holster. And then I saw it was an open-bottomed holster, and then I could see that there were expended rounds in there."

"Hmm," Bahr said, and that was about it for the interview.

10.

I sat at the kitchen bar while my wife, Imaging, was fixing breakfast. I looked out the window. The Grand Teton had pulled a thick blanket of gray clouds around itself. The moose were bedded down underneath the red willows.

"Take that!" Imaging said, her blue eyes laughing as she slammed cups of coffee down in front of Jim Leach and me. I began to sip and think. Leach sipped, too.

"What do they have on this kid, Catch the Bear?" Imaging asked.

"I haven't gotten into that much yet," I said. I wanted to talk with Leach about Bruce Ellison.

But Imaging persisted. "Well, what did they say at the preliminary hearing?" She'd been through murder cases with me before. "They had to have at least *some* evidence to bind him over for trial, didn't they?"

"Yes," I said.

"Well, what evidence was there?" she asked impatiently. "He's probably just a nice Indian boy who was in the wrong place at the wrong time."

"She's the attorney for the damned, Jim," I said to Leach. "She defends all the kids in our family and most everybody else's as well."

"I haven't heard a single thing against this boy yet," Imaging said. "You always go at a case backward." She broke some eggs into a frying pan. "How about some whole wheat toast?" She looked over at Leach, who only nodded. "If people could see how you study a case, it'd drive 'em crazy," Imaging said. "I think you should get to the first facts first."

"Sometimes you can see what's on top better if you study the bottom side first. I like to study bottoms."

"I know," she said. "That's corny. All right." She flipped Leach's eggs over. "What does Collins Catch the Bear say happened?"

"I haven't asked him yet," I said. "Collins wanted to tell me, but I wouldn't let him. "

"That's nice," Imaging said. "What does he say, Jim?" She shoved Leach's eggs toward him.

"Well," Leach began, a ponderous look on his thin face, "I'm not permitted to tell you what my client says without his consent. It's privileged under the law."

"Oh, yeah," Imaging replied. "I guess I knew that." Then she turned back to me. "I think you should know what Collins says before you take the case."

"Well, sure," I said, "but I don't want to know what he says just yet. I want to know what the rest of the evidence is first."

Imaging looked at Jim Leach, who was examining his toast skeptically. "I made that with pumpkin seeds, sunflower seeds, oat grits and millet, whole wheat flour, molasses, and milk—and I grind my own wheat. It's good for you. Eat it. You're too skinny." She put a jar of fresh red raspberry jelly in front of Leach. Then she left the room.

"What about the Bruce Ellison thing?" I asked Leach.

"What Bruce Ellison thing?" Leach asked.

"Well, to start with, he's your friend."

"Yes.

"And Collins Catch the Bear is your client."

"Of course," he said. "This bread's really good," Leach said.

"Both Ellison and Means were at the scene before the sheriff got there, and I know that the gun was put in Tollefson's hand by somebody. What if Ellison witnessed that?"

"I doubt that."

"What if he were called as a witness? He's not only your friend; he's your former client."

My questions about the Leach-Ellison connection weren't just mine. Judge Grosshans had questioned Leach thoroughly when he petitioned the judge to get into the case as Collins's attorney. After the judge had been assured that Leach was coming in at no cost to the taxpayer, he had further questions for him.

"Do you see the possibility of any conflict whatsoever between your prior involvement on behalf Mr. Ellison and your future work for Mr. Catch the Bear?" the judge had asked.

"Absolutely none," Leach had said. "I considered that question very carefully, because I think it is an important one, but I have absolutely no doubt in my mind there is no conflict."

"With all due respect to you, Mr. Leach, and don't take my comments wrong," Judge Grosshans had said politely, "and I'm not as knowledgeable about this case as you are, but you can understand—it troubles me a little bit."

Then the judge had turned to Rodney Lefholz and asked if the state had a position, and Lefholz said that the state certainly did: that he intended to call Bruce Ellison as a witness for the state against Catch the Bear, and since Leach had represented Ellison in the past, and since Leach would be required to cross-examine Ellison, an obvious conflict existed.

But Leach had already faced that sticky legal issue by obtaining a written waiver of the attorney-client privilege between himself and Ellison, which Leach said he'd be more than happy to file. He ended up by telling the judge, "Mr. Ellison understands, and I understand, and Collins and the public defender understand [that] there is no conflict between anyone I represent and Mr. Catch the Bear, and that is, of course, the way it should be."

Judge Grosshans questioned Collins, who'd been sitting quietly listening to this lawyer business. Collins answered the judge, saying he understood it all and agreed to Leach's representing him.

Back in my kitchen, I said to Leach, "Now, listen to this." I was quoting from the sheriff's supplemental report. "It says, 'Russell Means wanted White Bull and White Face and No Heart to present themselves as the only persons present at the shooting.' What do you think of that?" I told Leach there'd been at least fifteen Indians, maybe more, up there where Tollefson was killed, but Means was said to have selected just those three.

Leach didn't answer.

I broke the silence: "No one knows what Means did or ordered done at the scene *before* the sheriff finally got there almost three hours after Tollefson's death. Did Means or someone he directed find Tollefson's revolver on the ground near the open pickup door where the struggle between Tollefson and No Heart took place and put the gun back into the holster and then put the partially holstered gun into the dead man's hand?"

Leach listened.

I continued: "Lone Wolf told the grand jury that Means ordered him to wipe the prints off the door of the pickup, and Lone Wolf said he did. The FBI reported that there were no prints on the gun. Did Lone Wolf wipe the prints off Tollefson's revolver as well? Someone did. Otherwise how do you suppose a gun was loaded with six cartridges in the first place, put in a holster, then shot three times, and still there are no prints on it? Also, Tollefson was covered with blood to the very tips of his fingers, and yet there's no blood on the gun?"

Leach listened.

"That gun was *wiped* and then put in Tollefson's hand by someone who stuffed the dead man's finger into the trigger guard and forced the dead man's hand around the pistol grip. Could you make room for that proposition so we can discuss this problem a little bit further?"

"Maybe," Leach said.

"Now, suppose there was no funny business surrounding the revolver's ending up in Tollefson's hands. Suppose he was holding the revolver from the beginning, that he fell with it in his hand, kept hold of it with his finger inside the trigger guard as he fell, and that, by some miracle, not a drop of blood from his hand ever reached any part of the gun.

"Moreover, he had to hold the revolver in his hand not only to load it but to fire it three times, and thereafter he was holding it as he fell to the ground. But magically, he left no fingerprints. Not one. And magically, if he shot the revolver while it was inside the holster, it left no powder residue on the interior of the holster. This is the picture that someone wants us to adopt as fact."

Leach had stopped chewing his toast.

I continued: "Let's start with a simple question: In what direction does the cylinder move as it is fired?"

"Don't know," Leach said, seemingly without interest.

"I happen to know. It turns counterclockwise."

Leach nodded.

"That means that as the trigger is pulled, the cartridges moves to the *left*, bringing each unfired cartridge into place and so on, as the trigger is pulled each time."

Still no response from Leach.

"And in Tollefson's hand, as he lay there dead behind the pickup, which side of the revolver was up?" I asked.

Leach shrugged.

I slid one of the sheriff's photographs in front of him.

"The right side of the gun is facing up," Leach finally answered.

"Can you see the cartridge cases on the left side of the gun?" I asked.

"No. The left side's on the ground. The right side is up."

"Yes," I said. The empty cases were next to the ground. No one could possibly have seen those spent cartridges unless they picked the gun up."

"Oh!" Leach said, on the edge of exclamation.

"And do you remember what Bruce Ellison said about that?"

Leach thought for a long moment. Finally, he said, "No. I don't know if he said anything about it."

"Well, let's look at his statement again." I flipped to the page. "Here it is, and I quote: 'And then I could see that there were expended rounds in there.' Do you believe he could see that there were expended rounds in the revolver unless someone had picked it up?"

Leach looked puzzled.

"Remember, the empty cartridge cases could not be seen as the gun lay on the ground on its left side."

Leach was staring at the photographs. "Who picked the gun up?" he asked.

"That's the question," I said. "But of one thing I'm pretty damned sure: Bruce Ellison would never disturb a possible murder scene."

"I agree with that," Leach said.

"Someone—we don't know who—picked the gun up, opened the cylinder, and discovered the three spent cartridges. Then their prints as well as Tollefson's were wiped off the gun and the gun was placed in the dead man's hand and the gun was inserted partway into the holster. That's what makes sense here, don't you think?"

Suddenly Leach came alive, and all he said in a quiet whisper was "God—Jesus God!" Then he walked to the sun porch alone.

I looked at the photographs again. Blood covered the whole of

Tollefson's trigger finger. Even the fingernail was covered in blood. Yet no one, including the FBI, had reported finding any evidence of blood on the revolver, not even the most insignificant smear.

As for the gun and the holster: no fingerprints, no blood, no reported powder residue inside the holster. I thought the gun had been fired three times outside the holster and that, thereafter, it had been wiped clean of fingerprints, put into the hand of the deceased, and partially inserted into the holster. What person or persons were involved in creating this scene I did not know; nor was I willing to speculate.

When Imaging returned to the kitchen, I said, "Do you remember that character, Wambli No Heart, the black guy—you remember who I'm talking about."

"Yes," she said.

"No Heart now says he saw Collins shoot Tollefson in the back of the head with a .22."

"Well, I don't believe him," Imaging said. And she was usually right.

11.

Collins Catch the Bear walked ahead of me, stiff as an old stick, his orange jailbird coveralls flapping loosely over his bones. The deputy herded us into a small concrete-walled room in the Pennington County Jail. I heard the sound of steel on steel as the door slammed closed and the bolt locked into place. The deputy's footsteps faded down the hall.

I motioned to a metal folding chair in a corner of the room, and the young Indian sat down and looked up at me with the eyes of a small trapped animal. I pulled up another folding chair. Catch the Bear's lower jaw began to push out slowly, as if he were clenching his teeth. He folded his arms across his chest and spread his feet, as if readying himself to spring.

"How ya doin'?" I asked in a friendly voice.

He nodded.

"My name's Gerry Spence, I'm a lawyer. Maybe you've heard of me."

He nodded—a quick, staccato movement of his head, like a man agreeing because he had to. He was thin as a starved street cur, and his bare arms revealed no evidence of musculature. He would have had to eat a full dinner and drink a half gallon of water to make 120 pounds. Maybe he stood at five eight.

From long months in jail, his skin had faded to the color of custard. He wore plain black-rimmed glasses on a large nose that bent slightly downward from its middle, and his cheeks were high and flat. His straight black hair hung past his shoulders. I thought he looked like a Lakota should look in the bleakness of winter, except too solemn, too old for a boy of just twenty; his hide too faded. The single bulb in the ceiling glared down on his glasses. He kept his eyes on me.

"Did they bug this room?" I asked. He shrugged his shoulders. "Let's have a look," I said. The room held a small steel table upon which sat an old Underwood typewriter. I tipped up the typewriter and inspected its underbelly. Then I got down on my hands and knees and peered under the table. I felt the concrete walls with the palms of my hands. They had lately been whitewashed and were cold. The ceiling was flat and smooth.

I sat down and glanced at Collins Catch the Bear. I tried not to appear tough; I softened my eyes and opened up my face. Sometimes people are afraid of me. They have no cause. This is merely the way I look after putting on a tough expression all these years to cover my own fear.

"Well," I began again, with a new smile. "I'd like to get to know you. A lawyer ought to know his client."

He didn't answer. His uneasiness was contagious. I told myself he was only a kid.

I continued: "It must be pretty hard makin' it in a place like this," I said. His eyes didn't have that hollow look I'd seen in the eyes of killers, the look of a mirror when the silver has been rubbed off the back side so that the mirror's reflection is flat and dead.

Among the numerous papers and photos in the file Lefholz had furnished us upon a court order was a letter Collins had written to his sister. I thought the letter revealing:

Dear Sis,

Real glad to hear from you, it's been a while. My health is good and my spirits are not far behind. Proud to have a nephew and happy for you and Stan. My apologies for the last time we saw each other—to you and Stan both. Let my words and actions run away from me. Can't blame it all on fire water, as it didn't pour itself into my mouth.

Hope my apology will be accepted. Yes, Sandy has been writing, and it helps, and it also seems she is having hard times. Hate to hear that she feels like drinking at times. I know that none of her brothers have been setting anything that even resembles a good example. I have faith that she will come through all right.

My trial should be around the middle of January. My sights for it are neither high nor are they the lowest, real hard to say at the moment. Real glad you thought to write. You lifted my spirits a good deal. I'll close now so kiss your little one for his (bad guy) uncle and best wishes to Stan. I wish you a lot of health and happiness with your family and my respect comes along with it.

Take good care.

Collins

November 22, 1982

P.S. Kyle's picture was not in the letter.

"Well," I said, trying to sound easy. "It's hard to talk in a place like this. Wish we were sittin' on a log together on the edge of the woods someplace." I gave him another smile. I was almost whispering for fear the cold cement might bounce my words into unfriendly ears. "But let's see if we can find out some things about your case." I liked his solemn looks. Surely the jury would see that Collins Catch the Bear was no killer.

"I didn't belong in school," Collins suddenly began, as if to assert control of the interview. "I was the only one who wasn't white. The kids didn't understand. They hadn't seen an Indian before, and some called me 'the nigger.' I fought with some of the older boys. I didn't belong in that place—too many people. The McClain family lived in an apartment, and the city wasn't friendly." He talked mostly to the wall, his hands folded over his lap.

"I know," I said. "I've never seen the city smile, and the noises of the city sound like groans from a great sick beast that rolls over and belches out bad-smelling gases from its bloated belly."

Collins looked as if what I'd said surprised him. Who was this man talking nonsense like that?

"There are too many people there," Collins finally said.

"I've lived all my life away from the city," I said. "In the city, the people push and shove each other like they're corralled cattle."

"I didn't like it there with the McClains anymore," he continued, still speaking to the wall. "I didn't belong. I wanted to run. I was gone overnight, and they went out to look for me, but they couldn't find me, and then I came back the next day. I was twelve, and I ran away more than once, but I couldn't explain to them why I ran away."

"Can you explain it to me now?"

"I was lonely. But it didn't do any good to run."

"Yes," I said. "An empty heart in a small boy is very painful. But wherever the boy goes, the heart goes, too."

He nodded and looked to the floor.

"Maybe you were running *to* and not *from*," I said. "Maybe you were in search of your mother."

He continued staring at the floor.

I thought I could hear Catch the Bear's silent cry for his mother—and no answer. I'd been there: One night, my own mother walked out into my grandfather's orchard, lay down in a ditch, stuck my father's hunting rifle in her mouth, and, without saying good-bye, blew the back of her head off. The memory left me wordless but not free of the resurging pain.

We were silent together.

I saw the pain on Catch the Bear's face, and finally I was able to say, "Milwaukee was not a place to you."

"Yes," Catch the Bear said matter-of-factly, as if we'd returned from a world of nightmares. "I was lonesome in Milwaukee."

"Too far from your place," I said.

"Yeah, that was it," he said as if it were settled.

"Every living thing needs to have a place, and to be in its place," I said. "I know a story about that." He was patient and silent. It was I who needed to tell the story to break through the feeling of the macabre I'd created.

I began: "Old Tom Burlington lived all his life on the Shoshone Reservation in Wyoming, near Crowheart Butte. I lived for many years in that county. Old Tom's father and mother were among the first white people to settle there. He lived in a small one-room cabin by Dry Creek, a creek that was never dry and was filled with small brook trout. Tom always had a pot of strong coffee on his ancient woodstove—tasted like acid—and he usually displayed a couple weeks' growth of whiskers. His refrigerator sat outdoors on the front porch of his cabin. Tom said he couldn't stand the noise of it inside.

"No one could get old Tom to move away from his place, even when he was too old to take care of himself. Said he wanted to die right there. One night at his cabin, just the two of us were talking by the fire. 'I had me this pup, cute little fella with a natural bobtail,' old Tom said. 'Called him Bob for short, and a bunch a Denver dudes come up on the reservation one night and they stole Bob. He was just a bunch a fur and that waggin' bobbed tail, old Bob was.'

"'Then, in about three months, here come ol' Bob home again, all skin and bones, hardly growed none, and his feet was bleedin' and his eyes was as holler as that stump out there, but he come home, and he lay down by my feet and slept for a week, yes siree, by golly, you betcha. He slept fer a week, 'cept when I'd get up and go outside for something', he wouldn't let me outta his sight. This here was his place. And old Bob ain't never left since. Dog knows where his place is. Dog knows what a man don't know sometimes,' old Tom said." His old dog Bob was lying by the door to make sure he was there when Tom went out."

When I finished the story, Collins Catch the Bear only nodded and looked down at his hands. After a while he said, "When I ran away it hurt the McClains' feelings, and they worried, and they called the police. But when I came back the next day, they said they had to discipline me. 'Wash the dishes every night this week,' they said. 'You are grounded," they said. "You cannot go anyplace. You have to learn your lesson. You have to be punished for running away.'"

I said, "Maybe Milwaukee was a place to them, and they didn't understand that it was not your place."

"I didn't understand what was wrong with me," Collins said. "But I was lonesome for my people. I wanted to go back to the reservation. Don't know why I always wanted to go back to the reservation. It was the only place I knew, I guess."

Collins Catch the Bear leaned up against the cold, hard wall. Our long silences from time to time didn't seem to unnerve him. Finally, he said, "One time, the whole McClain family went on a boat ride on the lake. I was scared of the lake 'cause I couldn't swim, and I thought what would happen if the boat turned over and we were drowning in the lake? Then I knew that they would save their kids first and that I would drown, and I knew I didn't belong. I ran away some more, and I caused Mrs. McClain problems, wouldn't listen to her. I liked her, but I wouldn't listen to her."

I said, "It's not natural for a mother to take on a child who's not her own. Good mothers try, and many succeed. But it is not natural. At our ranch, we have a hard time making a cow who's lost her calf take on a calf who's lost its mother. Sometimes we pen 'em up together, but usually the old cow kicks at the strange calf. Sometimes you can skin the cow's dead calf and tie the hide to the new calf because it smells of her calf, but sometimes even that doesn't work."

"The McClains were good to me," Collins said. "They tried. But finally, they made arrangements for me to go back to the reservation, to the Community School."

I'd already read in the school's records that Collins didn't get along well there, either, and ran away. The word *love* never once appeared in the hundreds of pages of reports that chronicled this boy's life.

Love was a stranger.

I thought there should have been an order on the chart that read, *Attention all aides: Whenever you see this boy, please go over and hug him. And also, take him by the hand, go for a little walk with him. Enjoy yourself with him. He is a nice, bright boy. Have a good time with him. You, too, are entitled to a little pleasure in your work. Laugh a little. And love a lot. This boy needs a lot of love, and you aides need it, too. We all do. And don't forget to kiss him good night.* But the notes read: "This subject ran away again from the S.W. unit at 2:20 a.m. from the boys' upstairs middle bedroom window. Called police station."

Collins's black-rimmed glasses gave him a scholarly look, and he spoke slowly and calmly. He usually thought before he spoke, he was serious, and his voice sounded respectful and wise for such a young person patiently trying to explain himself to me.

He said, "I didn't like it at the Fort Yates dormitories, either. I'd been around all white people. Now I was with Indians, and it was hard for me to adjust to them. They were my people, but I didn't know them. And I couldn't speak their language." He stopped. Then he went on. "I was living in the dorms and I got to huffing."

"Huffing?"

"Yeah. That means smelling glue for a buzz. And they put me in jail one night when me and this other kid started a fire down on the river, and then they sent me to Jamestown, to the State Hospital, for twenty-one days, and the shrinks there just decided I had a bad upbringing; that was the problem."

"What was it like as a boy at the Jamestown State Mental Hospital?" I asked him.

"There were sick kids there. One kid would hit himself in the face all the time. He had sores and scabs all over his face from hittin' himself, and some of the kids just sat in a corner all day and rocked back and forth, and one kid would tell another kid to attack a person, and the person would attack, like a mad dog." He recounted this plainly, slowly, without emotion. "I was scared all the time I was there."

The hospital records reported that Collins was fourteen. They had him sign what was called a "treatment permit," duly witnessed, which supposedly gave permission to the North Dakota State Hospital to administer medication and to do "milieu therapy," whatever that was, and behavior modification, which I suppose included, in extreme cases, shock treatment and a frontal lobotomy. The permit gave authority for both individual and group therapy, all in accordance with the prescription of the hospital staff. The permit read, "The above procedures and possible risks have been thoroughly explained and are fully understood." No adult had signed the papers.

But when they examined Collins closely, they reported that "he had wax in his ears, that he has been fully toilet trained, at what age bladder and bowel control has been attained is not known." They found he had an above-average IQ, and the psychiatrist said that "Collins was essentially a lonely boy who didn't have any 'significant relationships,'" which meant, I suppose, that he didn't have any friends or family. They also reported that he cried a lot.

The nurses' notes said that when he was in the gym, he shot a few baskets, but when the other boys came, he sat down and only watched, that he always kept to himself and was often found alone, crying. The records revealed that Virginia McClain had searched for Collins, sent him letters, and when she finally found him at the hospital, she wasn't permitted to speak to him. Her letters were never delivered to him. So far as Collins knew, she had written him off.

But Mrs. McClain had told the school officials in a letter:

> It was very heart breaking for him and us to send him back [to the reservation], but we had to face the fact that everything we tried failed . . . We love Collins, and miss him, but his future is the most important thing to us..

I told Collins that Mrs. McClain hadn't abandoned him, that she loved him. "Mrs. McClain wanted to be your mother, Collins," I said.

He seemed not to hear me.

"She wrote you, but they didn't deliver her letters. Did you know that Mrs. McClain also tried to call you?" I asked.

"No," he said.

"They wouldn't let her talk to you."

"Why not?"

"I asked her the same question. She said they thought it would be best to take away from you what was very important—that way, they told her, you might behave."

"Oh," he said, as if he didn't understand. I didn't understand, either.

The nurse's notes read, "Collins seems homesick and is just waiting for the day when he can leave."

The hospital people had Collins write down what he felt his problem was, and he wrote in careful, correct penmanship, "I get in a lot of trouble." Under "Hobbies," he wrote, "Fishing, hunting." For "Dislikes": "Getting in trouble. Getting in fights." He couldn't think of anything to say under the heading "What people like best about me," and left it blank. Where the hospital's form asked, "What I think I'd like to do about my problems," he wrote, "I'd like to start over and see if I could do better." And where it read, "My plans when I leave the hospital are," he wrote, "To try to stay out of trouble."

I suspected Collins knew what they wanted to hear him say and he said it.

The hospital psychiatrist had at least provided Collins with a label: "Behavior disorder of childhood, unsocialized aggressive reaction 305.4." But there are no numbers in the psychiatric handbook for children crying for their mother, and no treatment called "love" was prescribed at the North Dakota State Hospital. Love is too scarce. The psychiatrist found that Collins's impairment was moderate to severe, and he recommended "that he be discharged to the Tribal Court for further disposition."

The tribal judge signed another paper that sent Collins back to the McClains in Milwaukee. Then Collins ran away again—running from that place crowded with whites, running to the place of his childhood, still running to find his mother, and knowing without knowing that there was no mother.

12.

Some men need a mate. And a qualification for matehood is the ability to share small things that will be forgotten tomorrow, fleeting feelings of joy and the dreams of the night before, such as when I come in for lunch and say, "I saw a tree swallow today—plain-looking little bird, dressed like a flying nun."

And Imaging says something like "Yesterday you wanted to know where the horses were in the horseradish, and today it's flying nuns." And we both laughed without laughing. I might choke on myself and die if I didn't have someone with whom to share small, irrelevant nothings.

I remember an old mountain man with whom I'd had little more than a passing acquaintance. We bumped into each other in the grocery store one day. His wife had recently been killed in an airplane crash—not the way for a mountain man to lose his wife. I told him I was sorry about his terrible loss, and suddenly he came bursting out with it: "I used to get up in the morning and I went to shavin' right off, and she'd holler up, 'How do ya want your eggs?' She knew how I wanted my damn eggs. I like 'em over easy. I been tellin' her that for almost fifty years now, and I always hollered back, 'I'd like 'em over easy, honey,' and then I'd go on shavin', and every morning it was like that—she'd holler up and ask the same thing, and now I still get up and shave, and sometimes I forget she's gone, and I keep waitin' for her to holler up and ask me how I want my damned eggs." And then the old man wept, and I wept with him.

Clarence Tollefson had been peacefully painting the house that morning and left a note to his wife before he left:

> Fertilized dandelions.
> Poisoned tomatoes.
> Garbage to dump.
> Shooting near Victoria.
> (1 mile)

Tollefson—Tully they called him—made little jokes all the time that people didn't always laugh at but silently appreciated, such as saying he poisoned the tomatoes and fertilized the weeds. Why not make small jokes?

But a person shouldn't have tried to push Clarence Tollefson around, especially on an issue of place, which had been the issue on the ridge above the camp when he was killed.

"This is our place, white man," the Indians had said,

"Show me your deed, then," Tollefson had said, and the Indians said their bodies were their deeds, like a coyote staking out his territory by wetting on a tree trunk—that was the coyote's deed, signed, sealed, and wetted.

What makes a place? A hole for a mole, the long prairies for the antelope. I thought of Tollefsen and the Indians again. The white men and the Indians had a bloody history of fighting over place. It was locked in their cells.

"This case is about *place*," I said to Leach. "Every creature will fight for its place."

For me, the kitchen is the heart of my place, like a lodge fire in the middle of a tepee. Kitchens, like the heart, should be near the center of the house and, like the heart, slightly to the left. Kitchens hold memories for me of the safe sounds and smells of mother and of the hungry boy, face flushed, still too young to sweat, hollering for a glass of strawberry Kool-Aid. It is a place for babes and men to be nourished.

"Nobody's home until they're in the kitchen," Imaging said.

The kitchen is the tribal meeting place where family members come stomping in out of blizzards and sniffing up to a pot of stew built around good neck meat and potatoes, with carrots and onions and garlic added and a pinch of parsley mostly for color. I've forgotten what else Imaging puts in hers, but the gravy comes out a good sort of brown and tastes slightly salty and is satisfying.

The place for the Lakota was the Black Hills, the Paha Sapa. The Lakota, too, were lashed to the past. They longed for the "old ways." They had their tepees, yes, but inside were stoves, and they drove cars, their Indian ponies only memories and white bones on the prairies. The Indians no longer jerkied their meat. They ate their food out of cans along with wienies and potato chips and chocolate bars. They drank firewater, cheap wine, and when they were not at the Yellow Thunder Camp, most lived in small shacks on the reservation. But the reservation was a place.

"How do you make this bread, Imaging?" Carole asked timidly.

"I got the recipe already," Leach said before Imaging could answer.

"He'll probably make it, too, when we get home," Carole said shyly.

"The hunters and the warriors are making bread nowadays, and the women have taken up the spear," I said. "People have their roles reversed."

"He likes to cook," Carole said of Leach.

I said, "He likes to chew the hides to make the moccasins, too, I suppose."

"That's simply an offensive statement," Leach stated. "Nobody scalps anybody anymore. We're out of the tepee."

"No," I said. "We napalm fields of innocent children, wipe out cities, turn millions to cinders with the push of one red button, and women can push buttons as easily as men." I didn't know what to make of my own argument. Sounded chauvinistic. Sounded like the mourning of some creaky antediluvian who was still hammered to the past.

"We are out of the tepees," Leach said again, busily chewing on Imaging's bread.

I liked to watch Imaging make bread in the kitchen, to see her get up on a stool to knead it because she's too short to stand on the floor and work the big, heavy globs of whole wheat dough on the countertop.

"Fresh bread is wealth," I said, "and I'm a wealthy man. Do the men bake bread in the Yellow Thunder Camp?" I asked Leach.

"That's different," he said. "They're trying to recapture the old ways."

"Ah, yes. There was a division of labor then. The men killed the enemy, and the women scalped them. And the women also made pemmican."

"The buffalo are gone," Leach said. "This is a different time."

"Well, maybe the Indians were regaining their old ways when they killed Tollefson. He was the white man, the enemy, standing over the camp looking down on the women and children. Wasn't it natural for them to kill their traditional enemy?"

Finally, Imaging said, "I never did understand what Tollefson was doing there."

Leach answered. "Tollefson told his girls' soccer coach, who's a psychologist, that he thought the camp ought to be blown off the face of the earth. He was real upset about the Indians. The psychologist said that it terrified him the way Tollefson talked like that, and he said Tollefson had a wild look in his eye."

"It was an issue of place," I said again.

The kitchen grew silent. I waited. Then I said, "A lot of the folks in Rapid City feel the same way as Tollefson—hating the Indians for taking over the National Forest."

"I think Tollefson was inviting trouble up there," Imaging said. "It takes two for a fight like that. That white man went up there into hostile territory by himself, with his guns, looking for trouble."

I pulled out the sheriff's report and began to read it aloud. "'Tollefson was an experienced gun handler and a good shot, his friend Ed Murphy said. Murphy had seen Tollefson at various times shoot a large-caliber pistol one-handed. Murphy said Tollefson was a man to hold his ground. He enjoyed the Black Hills and felt the national forest was a recreational area for both himself and everyone else. He was determined to go there and be where he wanted to be. Murphy advised that Tollefson would speak his mind. He didn't buy that the 1868 treaty gave the Black Hills back to the Indians. And he wouldn't back down in any conversation.'"

Leach said, "Tollefson liked to drive his four-wheel camper around, shoot turkeys, shoot targets and tin cans. At the same time, the Black Hills are sacred to the Lakota," Leach said, "like the Holy Land is to the Christians. How would the Pope and all the world's Catholics like it if the Indians set up a recreation center, a bowling alley, say, in St. Peter's Cathedral?"

"A lot of Indians are Catholic," I said.

"You can buy a Coca-Cola where Jesus walked," Imaging said.

"Christ ran the money changers out of the temple," Leach said.

"He didn't kill them," Imaging was quick to reply. She should have been a trial lawyer.

Leach said, "Tollefson was symbolic of the white culture

standing up there on a high place looking down at the Indian and threatening him."

"I should try to explain that to the jury as our defense, right?" I asked.

Imaging said. "It'll be an all-white jury, and they'll hate Collins, and it won't make any difference who killed Tollefson. Tollefson was killed by some Indian, and so that justifies the whites to kill an Indian—any Indian."

Leach walked out to the sun porch to take in the Grand Teton and to check out the landscape for the moose again. I followed him out, and we stood there together for a moment enjoying the winter scene.

"Beautiful," Leach finally said. He shook his head in awe. "You have it all."

"You ready to talk?" I asked.

"What about?" Leach asked.

"About what we don't like about each other."

Leach seemed surprised.

"I feel as if I've put you off," I began. "I've been trying for fifty years to improve—haven't made much progress. People seem to think I have a lot of power, and some are afraid of it."

He nodded.

"We're different," I said, "and what I don't like about you is that you won't share your feelings with me."

"I'm not used to saying what I feel. I'm not good at it," he said.

"I know. But I need to know how you feel. I trust feelings. In trying this case, I'll often be asking, 'What's going on? What are the jurors feeling?' Things happen in a courtroom in front of your face, and everybody else sees it except the lawyer who's doing the fighting. I'll need to know how the jurors are feeling. I'll be fighting. It's hard to see what's happening when you're fighting."

"Yeah, I know," Leach said.

"Are you ready to talk about your friend Bruce Ellison?" I asked.

"Okay," Leach said.

"What's going to happen if I get in the case and I have to attack Ellison to save Catch the Bear?"

"I talked to Bruce," Leach said, speaking to me like a son who wanted his father to believe him: "Bruce is a great man."

"I don't know him," I said.

"I talked with him a long time about this. I told him in the beginning that if I took Collins's case, that's how it would have to be. He agreed then, and he still agrees. Says he's only human—that he might not speak to me for a week or two if what I do hurts him, but what he was trying to say was that he understood. Bruce is at war, too, Gerry. He's in a battle for the Lakota. He'll lay it all down for them if he has to."

"I hope it doesn't come to that. I won't try to hurt him," I said. "But I'm not fighting for a cause. I'm fighting for one powerless Indian."

Leach nodded his understanding.

"If you're fighting for a cause, you can find yourself asking, 'Who is more important to the cause, Catch the Bear on the one hand or, say, the Lakota people?'"

Leach nodded.

"And you can find yourself arguing that Bruce Ellison is a decent man who has helped a lot of Indian people and who has the capacity to do a lot more good with the rest of his life, while the loss of Catch the Bear wouldn't be missed by many, if any."

Leach didn't answer.

"That's why I'm not a cause lawyer," I said.

Leach listened.

I continued: "You have a client. If you can't take advantage of every lawful break available for him, then you have to get out of the case. Cause lawyers are at war. They make their own rules like you would in war. They can sacrifice their clients, or themselves, whatever the cause requires. But I'm not at war. I'm defending one powerless Indian kid who is nothing to nobody."

"Bruce Ellison understands that," Leach said.

"And you're in conflict in another way," I said. "He's your friend, and Collins is your client. Which one has the right to your greater loyalty?"

"It's hard," Leach said, and the troubled look came back to his eyes. "But Bruce made it easy for me. He said I have to represent Collins."

"Can you do that?" I asked. We were both staring at the Grand Teton, which stood like a monument to the Sioux, to Wakan Tanka, "the Great Mystery."

"Yes, I can do that," he finally said, and his eyes grew soft. Then we walked back into the kitchen together, and I asked Imaging for another piece of her homemade toast.

13.

Collins Catch the Bear, this solemn, straight scarecrow dressed in prison orange coveralls, was sitting with his skinny young bones on a steel chair in that small, white concrete-walled visitor's room in the Pennington County Jail. I was sitting across from him. I took out my pen and notebook.

I began: "You're sensitive. You have feelings—you're maybe even a poet. I can hear it in your words sometimes. And you care. I know you can love, and you're bright. You can express yourself. What was going on with you?"

"All my brothers been in the joint, ya know. I guess I'm just like them," he said, as if blood were the cause of his current situation.

"What is the feeling you get when you ran?" I asked.

"Loneliness, maybe depression. People tried to care for me, but it wasn't like I was really wanted. I was being taken care of like any other responsibility—like feeding the goldfish or something."

When Collins ran to Mobridge, South Dakota, the place of his birth, he hid out in a home where they did a lot of drinking. But no place in Mobridge turned out to be a *place* for him.

"What to do with that Catch the Bear kid?" the tribal judge had asked. "He's failed everywhere. He ain't done nothing. If he done somethin', we could put him in the reform school. He's a hard kid to understand. Cries too much. Send him to Jamestown again. Only place left. They got more a them big heads there than we got here. Fix the papers up. I'll sign."

The records from Jamestown state that Collins Catch the Bear was seventeen, stood five foot seven and three-quarters, and weighed 118 pounds. "Has normal skin. Head—no dermatitis, and regular and symmetrical. Good eyes ears and nose. Mouth and throat in good condition. His chest showed no characteristic disease shape. His lungs were not in distress. His abdomen was flat. GI tract—no difficulty. His musculo-skeletal structure was strong, nervous system well coordinated, and he had no sensory deficit. His cranial nerves were intact."

But they did not examine the pain zone surrounding Collins's lonely heart.

"The patient stated he has been drinking alcohol and needs help. Apparently[,] patient has some insight as to what will happen to him if he drinks too much." The record reported, "He came from a family of eleven, four brothers and six sisters." (Collins was from a family of nine.) "Mother died from drinking alcohol in April 1976. Most of the children have been placed in foster home care.

"Patient is quiet, cooperative and compliant. He seems unhappy in this recent admission. He has less interaction with other residents in the unit. He seems to like reading a lot. No psychotic symptoms, hallucinations, delusions, looseness of asso-ciation, no gross disturbance in his thought processes"—which was to say, he was not psychotic.

The attending psychiatrist wrote in his report: "This is a 15 year old, single American Indian admitted today on an Indian com-mitment." (As we've seen, Collins was seventeen, but doctors are notoriously bad with numbers.) "He was doing well in school. He was well oriented, his memory was not impaired and his intelligence was about normal. His thought process was logical and coherent. His mood and affect were appropriate. His insight and motivation for treatment were questionable. He does not seem to realize what risk he takes when he takes drugs in the way he does. Impression: Drug addiction."

The record read, "Young male Indian who appears quiet and a little nervous about being here. Is cooperative with good eye contact."

The plan of treatment: "Orient him toward rules and observe his interaction with peers and staff—observe attitude towards structured living setting—will re-evaluate by 9-28-79."

The patient, Collins Catch the Bear, made the following statements, which are preserved in the record: "The reason that I came here is that I smoke too much marijuana. I was here three years ago. I smoked daily until a month ago, and now I smoke five joints a week. I was at the Youth Ranch about 10 months. I lived there because I didn't have any other place to go."

On September 21, 1979, at 3:54 p.m., Collins told one of the staff, "I'm frightened. I'm afraid I'm going to run away. I need my freedom."

The staff member went on to observe that "Collins is confused, anxious, and appears depressed. He expressed feelings of rejection and fear that we would just let him sit here for no reason. Responds well to psychological support."

Psychological support: a magical substitute for love that quits working at five o'clock sharp.

On September 23, Collins ran from Jamestown. There was only one place for an Indian to run: the reservation. Collins hitched a ride to Fort Yates in the back of a cattle truck, and of course the Indian Police found him. He was already drunk, and they threw him in jail at Fort Yates, where the walls were covered with the puke of generations of Sioux.

The tribal judge reluctantly signed papers that sent Collins to the North Dakota Industrial School in Mandan, North Dakota, the reform school. His crime: running away from the Jamestown State Hospital. No adult, no guardian, no attorney was present to represent him. Guardians and attorneys only cause trouble.

The admission form at the North Dakota Industrial School showed that Collins's mother was dead; that his older brother Clayton was in prison; that his older brother Anthony, who had been chosen over Collins by the aunt, was in prison; and that his half brother, Stanley No Heart, was in prison as well. The sisters were in different foster homes in Mobridge and Pine Ridge, South Dakota, and in Fort Yates, North Dakota. Their father, a hopeless alcoholic, was reported to be somewhere in Wakpala, South Dakota.

At the reform school, Collins was subjected to more tests. One cannot criticize conscientious people for doing their work. His IQ was well above average. The tester remarked that "Collins could tutor other students, but he is extremely withdrawn. Several other people in Hickory Hall have commented that they have never seen another inmate who talks so little—a couple of residency counselors believe that Collins is highly prejudiced against whites—and won't talk to anybody but Indians. Often times he would become depressed and cry. He said he was mad at the court 'because they've been sending me to too many places.'"

Under the form's heading "Evaluation of Treatment Needed," the word *discipline* was scrawled in a crude hand, misspelled.

The counselor at the reform school asked, "Collins, don't you understand? You have to grow up so you can go out there on your own. Everybody has to grow up and get a job. You have to make your own way," she said. "That's all we want for you—to be independent."

But the Lakota did not *want* their children to grow up to be independent. The only people who must be independent are those who are banished from the tribe. Banishment is rendered for only the worst crimes, like murder. The Lakota wanted their children to belong, to stay with them, to learn the ways of the tribe, to be a part of the tribe's strength, to learn its wisdom, to follow the way of the elders as their way had come down to them from the beginning of their people.

On October 7, 1979, another student and Collins Catch the Bear took the middle pane of glass out of a door at the northeast end of Hickory Hall. The co-supervisor was returning with three students she'd taken to see a movie when she noticed the window-pane missing. Another supervisor made a quick head count and found that the two boys were gone.

The Indian Police had no trouble finding Collins back on the reservation and returned him to the reform school. Collins told the Discipline Committee:

> When I first got here[,] I was lonesome for my family, so I started thinking about running away. This other kid said he wanted to run away, too, so we started thinking about how to do it, and when to do it. Altogether we waited about a week before we actually did leave.
>
> It was a Sunday night about 9:00 when we got our shoes from the shoe room. We took out a window from the door and climbed out, and then we ran behind Hickory Hall and into the hills and circled around the southern point of the school, crossed a highway and walked across some fields for a couple of miles, crossed another highway, walked south for a ways, then crossed the highway again and rested in a haystack until morning. Then we started hitchhiking for about a mile when Tiny [the cottage director at the North Dakota Industrial School] stopped and we got in his car.
>
> When we got to Mandan and stopped at a red light I

jumped out and took off running behind some buildings by a railroad track. Then I went into Taco John's, bought a burrito, and then I went over to the Red Fox Restaurant and had a coke, and then at a gas station I caught a ride to Ft. Yates. I stayed at Ft. Yates about a week with a friend's family. Then I went down to Wakpala, where my father is, and I was there for about a week before they caught me. They took me to the Ft. Yates jail. I tried to run when we got to Ft. Yates, but they caught me and held me in jail for six days. Then they brought me back up here today. I intend to stay here until I'm released, and I'll try to find my problem and get rid of it.

The Discipline Committee recommended that Collins meet with Dr. Lawrence, the superintendent. "We also think Collins should get involved as soon as possible in school, in recreation and in whatever we have to offer." Collins promised the committee that he wouldn't run away again and would start getting "involved." He said he would like to work with Elizabeth Houle, and she was assigned to talk to him on a daily basis.

On November 30, 1979, Elizabeth Houle reported: "Collins is starting to come out of his shell. He talks more in groups and gets involved in discussions. Collins is a positive student to have in groups. He isn't quite sure of where he wants to go in the future."

Other reports followed: "Collins is doing well. He needs glasses. He helps other students with their jobs. He gets no mail and is a very lonely person, but realizes he has to make it on his own when he gets out."

On January 22, 1980, the school reported that because Collins would be a legal adult, eighteen in July, it was recommended that he "go on independent living." An opportunity arose for him to attend the Young Adult Conservation Corps (YACC) in Mobridge, South Dakota; it was decided that he would be released after having been in the reform school for about five months. The file ended by saying, "It is recommended that future offenses committed by Collins Catch the Bear be considered in adult court," a sterile way of saying he should be treated like any adult male—and sent to prison.

Collins returned to Fort Yates and lived with the family of his friend Curtis Spotted Horse for about a year and a half. He and Curtis roamed the reservation drinking, and during the night of March 28, 1981, the two got drunk and broke into a bar in Aberdeen, South Dakota, wanting more liquor. They were caught inside, charged with third-degree burglary, and did nineteen days in the Brown County Jail. It was Collins's first offense as an adult, so he was given probation on the condition that he go to the Human Services Center in Yankton, South Dakota, for alcohol treatment. Curtis left before finishing the program, but Collins finished it.

Then, in October, Collins broke into another liquor store, drunk again. He was sent to the Federal Correctional Institution at Englewood, Colorado, to serve a term for larceny with an indeterminate sentence of zero to six years.

In the spring of 1982, the parole board sent Collins to the Friendship House in Rapid City, a halfway house outside the penitentiary and close to the Yellow Thunder Camp, which was practically on the edge of Rapid City. Collins later reported that with only a couple of months to go at the halfway house and soon to be released, something happened to him.

Maybe it was the spirits ruffling up his feelings like the wind does the feathers of the sage grouse in the springtime.

Maybe it was a heart that was so nearly empty it threatened to stop beating.

Or maybe it was because James Jones Jr., aka Wambli No Heart, who had escaped from Englewood and was residing at the Yellow Thunder Camp, had sneaked in to see Collins at the halfway house. The two had been friends at Englewood.

Jones told Collins how spiritual Yellow Thunder Camp was, how beautiful. No drinkin'. No dope. And the people were beautiful, and the children were innocent and beautiful, and the spirits were blessing the place. It was a *place*, and Collins should leave the Friendship House.

But no, Collins said. He would wait it out—just a little time to go for his parole—and No Heart could not talk him into leaving.

Jones, a black man, had tried to become an Indian. Collins said, "One time I told him about one of my half brothers, who is half black and half Indian, and Jones started playing the part of my half brother, whose name is Stanley No Heart, and Jones took on the name No Heart, which was my mother's maiden name."

Jones told Collins that his sister had been raped by a white boy, and a white man had stabbed Jones. He said his black father, drunken and crazy, had beaten up his Indian mother, and that his father had been killed by a white man. He said that his mother, who Jones claimed was a full-blooded Cherokee, was shot down by the white police.

"There's them DC niggers," Jones said, "and they group up, you know, and act real tough, and six of 'em were standin' on the steps at lunch one day, and the biggest one come up and kissed me on the neck, which is a sign that he was gonna make me his boy, and I pulled out my shank and stuck it into the bastard's stomach and then up further, and I killed the bastard." After that, Jones said he got life and was in all the federal joints.

He told Collins that later on he became gay because at Lompoc, a federal prison in California, he met this "transvestite" who initiated him. They sold themselves for whatever they needed: drugs or whatever else. "But I didn't make it with anyone but Indians. You should know that," Jones insisted. "I lived true to the brothers and gave them whatever they wanted because they were Indian."

Maybe it was because Jones told Collins all this that Collins felt the man's pain, and believed him. Then, the night before Jones left Englewood, Collins said Jones "tried something on me."

Collins told me, "We were in my cell, and he had some marijuana, and we smoked a joint or two. I was sitting on my bed, and he sat at my desk, and he started coming on to me, blinking his eyes and stuff, making a move on me. And he told me he was planning to take off. He said, 'You should come, too,' and I said, 'No, I'll wait. I'm about out of the joint, and I'll stay,' and he said, 'Okay, but before I leave, can I satisfy you?' I said, 'What do you mean by that?' And he said, 'What do you think I mean?' And his voice was real soft, like he was imitating a woman, you know, and I didn't like the idea.

"I was high, and I told him I didn't want to be satisfied, and we argued right up till count time, which is ten o'clock, and after that he came back and asked me if I'd smoke another joint with him, and so I did, and I sat at the other side of the room, and he got real mad and said, 'What's the matter? Don't ya like me no more?' like he was trying to be my girlfriend."

With only a couple of months left before parole, Collins decided to run once more. He said he was being harassed by another Indian inmate at the Friendship House, harassed until he couldn't stand it. He said the man put a hex on him, stuck a crow feather in his pillow, which is very bad, like death. The crow feather can bring worse than death, and the man wrote signs in mud on Collins's locker door. Bad hex. Collins said he had no choice but to run.

I looked at Collins like a man does when he doesn't believe what he's being told but is too polite to say so.

Collins said, "Well, it's true. I ran to get away from that hex." He stole a bike parked nearby and peddled to the Yellow Thunder Camp outside of Rapid City.

I was still sitting with Collins in that small concrete-and-steel closet in the Pennington County Jail where he was waiting for his trial on a charge of murder. His face was waxen and old looking. His hair fell past his shoulders, and his orange jail suit hung on his scarcely fleshed-out bones.

"What is it you want, Collins?" I asked.

"I would like to just have a place to stay," he said in the same flat, distant voice.

I waited.

Finally, he said, "Well, I wish I could talk Lakota, my people's language, and I wish my sisters could be together and have a place—that we could be a family with each other. I been thinking about my case, and I have a good feeling about that—there have been a lot of people working hard for me."

"Why do you think all these people have been working so hard for you?"

"I think my case—well, it's about the Indian way. It happened at the Yellow Thunder Camp. The camp is important to a lot of people. It's important to me. This is redneck country—cowboys— and they'd like to shoot the people they don't like. It's about a lot more than just me. I'm charged with a very serious crime. I know I'm not guilty of what I'm accused of doing."

"You're charged with maliciously killing a white man—intentionally with premeditation," I said. "I don't think you're guilty, either. I think you are a pawn, if you know what I mean."

"I know what you mean," he said. "I didn't hate that white man. I just wish that the camp could go on, that it could go on for the Indians who need it." He looked sad.

When Imaging handed me my morning coffee, she asked what I was thinking, as she often did.

I sipped silently, looking down into the dark, steaming fluid. Finally, I said, "Tollefson was killed on the twenty-first day of July, which was the day Collins was scheduled to be released on parole from the halfway house."

"How do you explain that?" Imaging asked.

"It's the spirits," I said.

14.

James Lee "Wambli No Heart" Jones told the sheriff his new story in an unemotional, business-like manner. A youngish blond lawyer named Gary Jensen sat beside him. The lawyer wore a three-piece business suit and sat relaxed and confident, with the air of a successful litigator. He was a friend of Rodney Lefholz. A federal marshal was also present, and while the sheriff's tape recorder was running, somebody offered Jones a cigarette, like a friend, and somebody else lit it for him. Jim Leach had copies of the tapes in a file.

Jones said that Russell Means had appointed him chief of security at Yellow Thunder Camp, and that just before Tollefson was shot, Moses Fast Horse from Wounded Knee had hollered down to Jones. Jones said he looked up to see the white man standing two feet from the flagpole there on the ridge. Jones said, "I ran up—probably on the footpath east of the cliff—and by the time I got there, some other men from the camp had already arrived. I asked the white guy, 'What are ya doin' here?' And the white guy said, 'Nothin'. Just lookin'. Just tryin' ta relax a little.' And then I said, 'What are you doin' looking down on our camp?'"

Jones said Tollefson was sitting in his pickup by then, and the driver's door was wide open. He said Evans White Face was on his right, and Smokey White Bull was on his left, and by then there were other Indians surrounding the pickup. Both windows in Tollefson's camper were rolled completely down. It was half past noon, and it was a clear day.

Jones said, "I told the white guy, 'Move on out of here. This is our land, this here is our home—our camp.'"

"I got a right to be here. This is National Forest land," Tollefson said.

"This here is our place, white motherfucker," Jones said somebody hollered. "Get yer white ass outta here." He said another Indian pounded his fist on the roof of Tollefson's pickup, making the white man jump.

"Ya wanna see what this camp looks like? Well, why don't ya come on down the right way—like a white man, and go through security," Jones said.

"I don't have to go through security," Tollefson said. "This is National Forest. I got the same right to be here as you."

"That's bullshit," somebody hollered. "This is Indian land."

Jones said there were other Indians standing behind him, facing Tollefson, and some of the Indians had knives.

According to Jones, Evans White Face hollered, "Move off this land," and everybody else was shouting obscenities. "Everybody around the vehicle was in an uproar and using 'verbal language,'" as Jones described it.

Then Jones said Smokey White Bull got to hollering about the 1868 treaty and how the whites had broken it. "That's what you white motherfuckers did before. You gotta get off this land. This is our land!" And the "conversation" went back and forth, Jones said. But Tollefson said he didn't believe in the Treaty of Fort Laramie.

In black and white, the 1868 treaty had promised the Black Hills to the Indians. The Indians were guaranteed:

> the absolute and undisturbed use of the great Sioux Reservation. No person shall ever be permitted to pass over, settle upon, or reside in the territory without the consent of the Indians . . . and no treaty for the cession of any portion or part of the reservation shall be of any validity or force unless executed by at least three-fourths of all the adult male Indians occupying or interested in the same.

And the Indians had agreed:

> never to attack any persons at home, nor molest the wagon trains nor capture or carry off from the settlements white women or children,and they will never kill or scalp white men, nor attempt to do them harm.

The treaty was ratified by Congress and signed by President Ulysses S. Grant in 1869, but it rankled some in Congress. It was the only instrument of unconditional defeat ever signed by the U.S. government and ratified by Congress.

Clarence Tollefson was not impressed with history. This was still the National Forest, which belonged to everyone.

"Everybody kept yelling at Tollefson," Jones said. "He probably was scared, surrounded by fifteen guys," and Jones claimed the argument went on for twenty to twenty-five minutes.

"I could see fear in the man's face," Jones said. "When he was talking, his head was kinda crooked, and he held his cheek with his hand," and then Jones said Tollefson reached over on the seat right next to him, picked up a gun in a holster, and started swinging it toward Jones, Evans White Face, and Smokey White Bull, who were standing at the door.

"Collins Catch the Bear had moved around on the passenger side and laid his rifle on the window sill where you push the lock button, and the barrel was about a half inch from the inside," Jones said. "This Tollefson didn't want to move aside, and I told him I would drive him down, because if he didn't move[,] trouble might start, and it didn't make no sense to see trouble up there, and he still didn't want to move, and by then there was a lot of slang and verbal language, like, ah, 'white motherfucker move away from this land,' and then he went for his gun. I thought it was a .22 pistol."

Jones continued: "I was standing in front of him, that's where I got the black [gunpowder residue] from. When he had the pistol in his hand, I was completely in front of his face. His head was coming around toward me, and his eyes was rolled up back in his head like he was tuned, and he started reaching for the pistol, and as the pistol was coming up into the air, comin' around—the shot went off.

"I can't say that I seen the bullet come out through his mouth. I could say I seen the smoke come from the gun, and as the smoke come from the gun, I seen a bunch of blood come from his mouth and through his nose, but I didn't see the actual bullet come out."

Then the deputy asked, "Did any of that blood spray on you?"

"No," Jones said. "I seen the trace—"

"The powder spray?" the deputy led.

"Yeah."

"And I seen the blood coming out the man's nose and mouth. I was standing directly in front of him."

"Okay. Okay. The shot went off, and then what did you do?"

"When the shot went off, everybody just broke and ran. [Tollefson] just rocked back and forth. As we was running we heard two shots, and like I say, we wanted ta get in a position so we wouldn't be fired at, and when we didn't hear no more shots, I immediately went down to the kitchen to get all the women and children and have them taken back into the creek area so they wouldn't get hurt."

The deputy said, "Now, I want to go to the shots. You heard the shot that Collins Catch the Bear fired?" he said, leading the witness again.

"Yes."

"How many more shots did you hear?"

"Me, personally—I heard about two more shots—could have been more, but I heard two," Jones said.

He continued on like a bored reporter reciting the evening news: "Two women went in to get Russ [Means]. Drifter had been up on the ridge and Rudell, and Yellow Cloud, and Bear Shirt, and Omaha John and Skip[,] and pretty soon Russell Means come there and Nick Meinhardt, and Tom Gammon.

"And Russell Means come to me and asked what happened, and I looked at Smokey. And Means said, 'I already asked him. I want to hear it from you,' and there was so many people around me[,] and right off the bat I didn't want to spill the beans on Catch the Bear, so I just told them the man shot hisself. So, we went over to where the man was lying there, back of the vehicle on the passenger side, at the end, facedown to the ground with the gun and holster still in his hand, and blood was all over the ground.

"Russell Means asked if anybody touched anything, and I said, 'Well, I opened the door,' and Means blew up and asked me why I'd do that, and I wanted to tell him, but I didn't tell him because, you know, out there they got a motto—people don't snitch on each other. So, Means immediately told somebody to wipe the fingerprints off the door handle of the passenger side."

"Who?"

"Sam Lone Wolf went over and wiped it off—took a little gravel from the ground, spread it over the door, blew the excess dust off, and after that, Bruce Ellison and Jan [Hamil], which is another Black Hills attorney, come up."

Jones said Means told everybody they'd have to go in and give statements to the sheriff, and a couple of the men said they couldn't go in because the sheriff had warrants on them, and Russ agreed. "So, he narrowed it down to Smokey White Bull, Evans, and me."

"Okay," the deputy said. "Now, at this point he [Means] is telling everybody there that they are not to talk to law enforcement except you three?"

"Right."

"Did anybody else, and I emphasize *anybody else*, say this?" Here in the recording, my feeling was that the deputy was trying to remind Jones to connect Bruce Ellison to the alleged cover-up.

"After Bruce Ellison came up there, he advised everybody to remain silent."

"Not to speak to any law enforcement?" the deputy led.

"Yes, that they have the right to remain silent—or they can give their name and, ah, birth date."

"He called you one by one?"

"One by one."

"And he give us our rights, as far as what the law was, to remain silent, and we didn't have to say nothing, just tell exactly what we seen, and so after that we just waited till law enforcement come up."

"And did you tell Bruce Ellison what happened?" the deputy asked.

"What I told Bruce was the same thing I told Russ—that the man shot hisself."

"That you blocked the—" the deputy led.

"I blocked the gun as it was coming down, and the man shot himself."

"When law enforcement arrived was Collins Catch the Bear up there?"

"Collins Catch the Bear stayed away until that night. That's when the women and children were called out from the creek area."

"When you was up on the ridge," the deputy asked, "did you hear any comment by anybody stating that that vehicle had been there before?"

"I heard Jan say that she seen that vehicle down at the firing range before."

The deputy led Jones some more: "Okay, when you were at the door of the vehicle talking with the individual, you saw Collins Catch the Bear go around the vehicle with the .22 rifle, is that right?"

"Yes."

"Okay. And then he laid the .22 rifle on the doorsill with the barrel just barely inside the vehicle, right?"

"Yes."

"Okay, now just prior to the gun going off were you able to see Collins Catch the Bear?"

"He was directly in front of me."

Considering the sharp downward path of the bullet, Catch the Bear would have to have been standing on a stepladder when he shot Tollefson, but the deputy did the best he could: "Did Catch the Bear raise that weapon up?" he asked.

"When the weapon was fired, he just barely came up—off the windshield [he must have meant windowsill]—just kinda like this." This was the best the deputy could get from Jones. Then the deputy quickly moved on to another subject.

"Okay. Did Collins Catch the Bear say anything at this time?"

"No," Jones said.

"Had he said anything prior to that?"

"Yeah. He was one of the ones using foul languages on the dude."

"Okay. But from the time he laid the gun on the windowsill to the time the shot went off, did he say anything?"

"He said something before the shot went off, but he didn't say nothing when the shot went off."

"What did he say when the shot went off?"

"Oh, he was telling the dude that he's—he's tired—"

The deputy interrupted Jones. "You say he's telling the dude—"

"He's telling him, he said, 'White motherfucker, I'm tired.'" Jones finally got the words out. "'Tired of you guys messing with Indians. Now, get off this fucking land.'"

"Okay. And at that point the shot went off?"

"At that point as the dude's pistol was coming up into the air around—the shot went off."

(If, indeed, Collins was even there, Jones's answer to the deputy provided Collins with a defense: that he had shot Tollefsen *in defense of another*, namely, James Lee "Wambli No Heart" Jones, or even in self-defense.)

"Okay. The shot went off. And you could see the smoke—" the deputy led.

"The smoke coming from the . . ." Jones hesitated.

"Coming from the rifle of Collins Catch the Bear. Okay? When the shot went off, everybody ran, but you stayed for a moment, evidently." The deputy was still leading.

"When the shot went off, nobody ran. Only until the blood came out his nose and mouth; that's when everybody broke."

Later, Jones said that Collins gave him the rifle, which belonged to Tom Gammon, and Jones hid the rifle near a tepee, buried it about two feet down. He drew the deputy a map of where the gun was hidden. Jones told the deputy there were all kinds of firearms hidden in the camp: .357 Magnums, shotguns, a sawed-off .22, and a high-powered rifle.

"Russell Means gave the order for everybody to bury everything. Means has a .22 pistol and a .357 he kept in his dresser inside his tepee, but I think they're buried."

"Do you have knowledge of any dynamite in the camp?"

"I seen, ah, Russell Means, ah, with dynamite in his hands. But I can't say where it's at."

Then Jones said he'd overheard conversations about a mysterious group of highly skilled, trained men "who were going into Governor Janklow's territory to kidnap Janklow and take him to Bear Butte 'cause the Indians didn't like what they're doing to Bear Butte—letting tourists tromp all over the Indian's sacred mountain."

The deputy wanted to know where this certain group came from, and Jones said, "AIM has dogs"—referring to "dog soldiers"—"and three days after I got to Yellow Thunder Camp, the place was loaded with dog soldiers in camouflage uniforms an' they were carryin' Mini-14s, M16s, and I seen one AK-47."

"And, okay, you saw these dog soldiers in camp?"

"Yeah. They was outside the camp, behind the trees, using walkie-talkies. I counted sixteen. They had canteens, and they was ready."

Jones told the deputy that he finally told Russell Means the truth. He said, "They were having the Feast of the New Moon, and the children were given presents, and Russell Means was sitting down by the kitchen with his wife. I went over an' asked him, 'Could I speak to you for a minute when you get time?' And I walked over to the garden, and in about three minutes he come over, an' I told him, 'You know Catch the Bear killed that white man over there?' An' he said, 'Oh, no,' an' he said, 'You keep your mouth shut. Now we got big trouble.'"

Jones said, "Means told me ta leave out of my story the part about me openin' the door to the car—to just say the man shot himself. Means told me an' Evans an' Smokey not to worry 'bout nothin' cause he'd beaten six or seven murder beefs already. That's the onlyest thing I can remember," Jones said. "Onlyest thing."

Then Jones told the deputy about a later conversation he had with Bruce Ellison over the phone from jail, after he had supposedly been arrested—I use "supposedly" here because I thought Jones was a snitch from the start and that the feds were covering for him by arresting him.

Jones said he told Ellison, "This guy [Tollefson] was shot from a distance, and I let Ellison know that I wasn't gonna be charged with no murder beef, and Ellison told me, 'They're up to their old tricks. You have a right to remain silent, and don't worry about nothin'. Yellow Thunder's right behind you.' And then I went back to my cell and got to thinking about this shit, and I thought they was using me, you know, and I got to thinking, I'm the one that'd be put on the hot spot. Collins was the one they'd let go because he's one of their own, and I'm not going to be—"

At this point, the deputy helped him again: "You were getting the feeling you were being set up?"

"That's the feeling I was getting, 'cause I'm not Indian, you know, with long black hair. Because I already done time, you know." Then he said he told Gary Jensen, the young blond lawyer appointed to represent him, what had actually happened. After that, Jensen "cut the deal" with the state and the feds so that Jones would get immunity in exchange for his testimony against Collins Catch the Bear. Finally, Jones said, "This Collins Catch the Bear, if he was even apprehended, he'd tell on his own self. I know that for a fact. In due time he would. His life wouldn't be in danger if he told on his own self."

15.

The next morning, Imaging was sitting on a small wooden stool sipping her first coffee and gazing with early eyes out the kitchen window to the quaking aspens to the south. Jim Leach and his friend Carole were not up; nor was the sun, but it was already light, and the trees were naked. You could tell the morning was cold by the subzero haze that hugged low on the snow.

"I've been thinking about Catch the Bear," Imaging said. "How can the state try to convict someone with a witness like Jones?"

"It's the state's business to convict," I said.

"It is not their business to convict. It's their business to do justice. You've always said that." Then she sipped some more coffee. "What does Catch the Bear say about this Wambli No Heart?"

"They were friends," I answered. "Jones liked to play Indian, hung out with the Indians in prison, and after he got to know Collins, he took his mother's last name of 'No Heart.'"

"Isn't that nice?" Imaging mused, sipping from her cup and looking out at the barren winter aspens. "A man takes your mother's name and then accuses you of murder."

"Wambli No Heart was supposedly an escaped murderer from Englewood."

"How can they use an escaped murderer's testimony?"

"It's the commerce of justice," I said. "Men trade in justice, barter in it and make deals," I said.

"What kind of deal did this No Heart make?"

"Lefholz and the feds gave No Heart immunity for everything past and present in exchange for his testimony that Collins shot Tollefson in the back of the head with a .22."

"You mean they can't prosecute him for Tollefson's murder even if he was the one who killed the man?"

"Right," I said. "And they gave No Heart Jones immunity for all other crimes committed by him at the Yellow Thunder Camp. He even got immunity for escaping from federal prison."

"That's justice!" Imaging said.

"There's more. No Heart Jones hit the jackpot. Lefholz, on behalf of the state, and the U.S. attorney, on behalf of the feds, agreed to go to the parole authorities and get Jones paroled on the murder charge he'd been serving—get him a new identity, put him in the fed's Witness Protection Program. He not only got a new name, but they agreed to concoct a new history for him. He'll get a new Social Security number, a new set of fake recommendations from employers who've never hired him—whatever he needs for a brand-new life."

"That's such dirty business," Imaging said. "But who'd believe this so-called Wambli No Heart anyway?"

"About any white juror in Rapid City," I said. "It's war out there, and in war it's the scalp count that's important."

"Well, you'd better get the venue changed," Imaging said.

"That's up to a white judge, former prosecutor himself, Judge Grosshans, and he's already turned down Leach's motion for a change of venue, and he turned down the public defender's motion before Leach got on the case. Why wouldn't he turn me down?"

"Uh-oh," Imaging said. "You do have trouble." She continued sitting on her little stool and looked out at the trees.

After the killing of Clarence Tollefson, James Lee "Wambli No Heart" Jones hung around the camp until he was finally arrested. I couldn't understand how a lately escaped seasoned con would simply sit by waiting to be recaptured unless he was a government plant. And he was only a month away from parole when he supposedly escaped from Englewood. And then he just happened to surface at the Yellow Thunder Camp? Why would a man who'd spent thirteen years in federal penitentiaries and who was only one month away from being freed on parole give it all up to go to Yellow Thunder Camp—unless, of course, he was, indeed, a plant who'd been promised a deal?

I reviewed the written agreement between the State of South Dakota and the federal government, as one party, and Jones as the other. It contained the usual recitations: that "Jones sincerely believed his life would be in jeopardy because of retaliation by members of Yellow Thunder Camp and supporters thereof." The agreement provided that in return for Jones's cooperation, the State of South Dakota and the United States of America were willing to take the necessary precautions to protect the well-being of Jones (which is their duty for every citizen anyway). Simply stated, the agreement made it appear that to save his own life, Jones had come forward with the truth.

I knew before I faced Jones in court what his story would be: that he'd lied in his first statement only out of fear for his life. Under the agreement, Jones agreed to testify "before any grand jury, court of law, or other tribunal," which was to say that he had to tell his new story against Catch the Bear whenever and wherever the state or feds wanted.

The government's program to implicate Means and Ellison in criminal conduct was likewise amply provided for in Jones's agreement. It called for Jones to testify "on all cover-up or obstruction of justice cases surrounding the shooting of Tollefson. And Jones agreed to testify to the existence of firearms and contraband at Yellow Thunder Camp, the harboring of fugitives at Yellow Thunder Camp, and any and all other criminal activities carried on at Yellow Thunder Camp."

The war against the American Indian had never ceased. And one of the principal weapons in this (and any war) remained the same: the treachery of a turncoat. So it was that even the faithful Little Big Man had helped deliver up his chief, the great Crazy Horse, to his white captors.

The servants of white power, I believed, had enlisted one James Lee "Wambli No Heart" Jones to betray a camp of Lakota Sioux and its leaders, after which white power would smash the camp under its collective boot heel like so much vermin, along with one frail, frightened young Indian named Collins Catch the Bear.

16.

Eddie Moriarity, my partner of many years, sat in my office with a grave expression on his face. Eddie has solid Irish looks. He isn't a large man, but he has the appearance of much larger men—husky, with a heavy, dark brown beard. He is the kind of person one liked to take into tough places, places where you needed your flank protected. I'd taken Eddie Moriarity into many.

Eddie is also a brilliant tactician, a general who could think calmly and clearly in battle, even with the enemy's hands around his throat, and he has an Irish way with people. It's not exactly blarney, but close, and Eddie is easy to like. People trust him, and that includes lawyers who are his traditional opponents in that pit called the courtroom.

I sometimes claimed that the man was damned near illiterate, which is not to say he isn't educated, articulate, intelligent, or thoughtful. But he mutilates the English language. His is the speech of miners and other hardworking men. In Eddie's world, if a man could make himself understood, that was enough, and you didn't have to listen very hard to understand men, their faces blackened, coming up out of a copper mine. And in the courtroom, one had no problem understanding Eddie Moriarity.

I sent Eddie ahead of me in important cases to scout things out, get the lay of the land. I relied on his assessments. Eddie could see things I often never saw, and he could puncture the thick hide of a case right to the jugular. In important cases, I liked to have him by me in the courtroom, thinking one step ahead of me and fighting to protect my rear.

It helped that judges liked to listen to Eddie. In the appeals courts, where judges sit somberly, dressed in black like high priests, listening to endless strings of the lifeless words that make up lawyer talk, sounds that must bore them until their toes curl, Eddie would come in with his good Irish smile, a slight peace offering to the judges. His palms up, open and innocent, and with a twinge of embarrassment on his face, he was like a schoolboy who wants to say something important but is a little nervous, but who makes you want to hear him. In your heart, you are urging him on. Then, suddenly, out of Eddie Moriarity would come the high, strained voice of a man in battle, the words he used, simple and powerful.

What he'd say to the judges was often soaked in passion. The judges' bored scowls would then vanish as Eddie beseeched them to have the courage of their convictions, to make the hard decisions the case required, as if saying, "You guys have got to take the bull by the horns . . ." And the judges would hear him because he spoke in the language of men, clean and honest, leaving the fine-honed legal arguments to be deposited in layer upon layer of intellectual mud by his opponents. Eddie Moriarity dealt in fresh blood.

Like any man, Eddie felt fear, but he also loved a good fight. It's not that he would rather have fought, but it's almost like that, and although he sometimes struggled toward peaceful resolutions, it was hard for him because it was *his* fight, and he didn't want to give it up.

He was nourished by the adrenaline of battle. At times, I thought he was addicted to it.

And yet . . . in the case of Collins Catch the Bear, Eddie Moriarity was uncomfortable. He didn't trust Jim Leach. Leach was one of those "cause lawyers," Eddie thought. And Eddie had had his fill of cause lawyers, whose primary focus was the cause, not the client.

"I'm tellin' ya, ya gotta be careful o' that Leach," Eddie told me. "He's mixed in with that Ellison somehow, an' he's probably mixed in with Means, too. He's got a lotta those cause friends, Means groupies, and I don't like it, Gerry." His eyes were troubled.

I waited for him to finish.

He continued: "I'm not gonna let ya walk into some trap in South Dakota. Too damn far from home to get trapped," he said. "And how 'bout Leach? Has he made up his mind yet about which side o' the case he's on?"

"Yes," I said. "I've settled the matter with Jim. He's a good man, Eddie. He and I have had good talks. We've put it all on the table, laid it all out, and Jim's okay."

"Well, if you're sure . . ."

"I feel sure," I said.

"That's good enough for me," Eddie said, and he meant it. "You have a feeling for things like that." And from that point on he'd treat Jim Leach as his brother. Eddie Moriarity was that kind of man.

"But I can't figure out why we want in on this case," he continued.

"Well, it isn't the money, that's for damn sure," I said. Eddie knew that we wouldn't be paid a cent, and we'd have to bear our own expenses. In the end, like the Indian hunter, we'd either win and eat or lose and starve. Not only that, but our tribal members, our secretaries and investigators, all wanted to eat whether or not we won, and our rent and taxes still accrued. There were no comfortable salaries coming to us from the government or generous retainers from large corporations or banks. Indeed, when bankers passed our law office, they crossed over to the other side of the street.

Then Eddie asked the right question: "I've been wonderin' what this case means ta you. It's got to be more than a just a case of an Indian kid charged with killin' a white man."

"It's historically symbolic," I replied. I could tell my answer didn't grab Eddie Moriarity. I pressed on: "This is a case that brings American history up to date with the Indian. The Indian has always been exploited by the white man. When Columbus first laid his eyes on the American Indian, he remarked what beautiful people they were. They were tall and strong and graceful. They seemed healthy, and were friendly. Then he gathered up a bunch of them and killed them, got them out of the way like chopping down trees that had grown up in the road.

"And the Indian nation has suffered a systematic extermination in America ever since. We've massacred them with bullets and disease and alcohol, killed off their buffalo and stolen their land. We've imprisoned them in holding pens called reservations and smashed their pride."

Eddie was used to my speeches.

I continued: "My opinion is Collins Catch the Bear is the white man's symbol of what little power remains of the Indian culture. In my mind, the state and the feds have joined together with the same intent once harbored by General George Armstrong Custer. Custer pledged to exterminate the last remaining cells of Indian resistance. They want the scalp of one small Indian named Catch the Bear. But wouldn't it sweeten their days to wipe out not only the Yellow Thunder Camp, but Means and Ellison along with it?"

"Makes me mad," Eddie said, rubbing his thick beard between his thumb and forefinger.

"The power people in South Dakota have hated Indians for a

hundred years. It's a part of their history, like the Irish hating the Protestants, something like that." I gave him a knowing look.

"Well, that's all well and good," he said. "And I'm all for the case, don't get me wrong, but there's hate ever' place. I mean we can't take a case and cure hate. We're a history of race haters, and ya can't cure it in a single case, or a hundred. And remember: we're not cause lawyers."

"Right," I said. "But what makes it more frustrating to me is that the Indian is sick and tired of also getting fucked over again by white do-gooders. I mean, it was enough when the whites broke the treaties and annihilated a whole culture. But the Indians had to face a second wave: the white churches who wanted to convert them to a foreign religion and the sociologists and anthropologists and pointy heads who wanted to study them and 'help them' by converting them to the white man's ways. Maybe worst of all are the weepers and the criers who blubber and sob about the terrible plight of the poor American Indian, while most Indians are sick of us and don't want our help."

"Okay," Eddie said. "So, you want to join up with the Indians in this case and go kill another Custer?"

"Well, no," I said. "All I want to do is save this one Indian kid"—and then I realized I'd left something out. "And have a good fight," I added.

"Yeah," Eddie said as if he understood. "Well, Gerry, it's a beautiful case. Let's go after it."

"Wait. I want to make another speech," I said to him.

He sat back in his chair and folded his arms as if to protect himself from the onslaught he anticipated.

"This case is about a young Indian who's lost his heritage. His veins carry Indian blood. His cells are the cells of the Sioux. He looks like an Indian, but he's lost his Indianness. He wasn't acceptable to white people, but he didn't belong to the Indians, either. He spoke like a white person but couldn't say a word of Lakota.

"He belonged nowhere, to no one. He had no *place*. Only the worst offenders, the murderers and traitors in a tribe, are ostracized from the tribe. Collins Catch the Bear committed no crime, but he had no tribe.

"Then, one day, he ran away as he had always run away. He ran, trying to leave behind the emptiness inside him. He didn't know where to run. He didn't know why he was running. All he knew was that he had to run."

Eddie was a good listener.

"He finally ran to the Yellow Thunder Camp. Suddenly, he felt a sense of place. These were his people, and the children were being taught the language of the Lakota. He could hear his native tongue being spoken, and the sounds of his ancestors grabbed at his heart. The camp was a sacred place to him, as all true places are sacred to us."

I paused to pull my thoughts together. "This is a case about a white man who wanted to drive the Indian from his last place. It's the universal struggle of all of us to find our place on this earth and, having found it, to keep it."

"I like the case," Eddie said softly, as if I didn't need to convince him further.

I handed him a file. "Take a look at this. Exhibit B." The file contained a news release authored by the prosecutor, Lefholz. He had sent it to the *Rapid City Journal*, and the paper had published it.

LEFHOLZ CALLS FOR FEDERAL ACTION ON A.I.M.'S YELLOW THUNDER CAMP

Attorney General candidate Rod Lefholz today charged the American Indian Movement's Yellow Thunder Camp is "nothing more than a haven for murderers and escaped convicts . . ."

Last week A.I.M. leader Russell Means asked for a congressional investigation of local law enforcement activities regarding the Yellow Thunder Camp. "This call for a congressional investigation is just a smokescreen to cover up the true nature of the camp," said Lefholz.

Lefholz said, "Until the camp is closed, all I can do is vigorously prosecute the murders and other acts of lawlessness that are connected with the camp."

"All South Dakotans, especially Indian people, unjustly suffer from the existence of Yellow Thunder Camp and the image created by it. Means, the self-proclaimed A.I.M. leader of the camp, himself a convicted felon, only wishes to serve his own selfish interests and not those of Indian people," said Lefholz . . .

"We've had enough violence and bloodshed. It's time for the Federal Judge to recognize the camp for what it is and put a stop to it."

"The power boys are playing politics with the case," I said to Eddie when he had finished reading it. "But Means is a politician, too. In his own way, he's a master politician. He knows how to make a speech. He's charismatic. AIM is a political movement, and so, all's fair in love and politics, isn't it?"

Eddie asked, "And so, everybody's in politics, aren't they? Everybody, that is, except us."

"The Indians don't have the weapons. The state and the feds have all the power. They have the media. The media rile up the people against the Indians, breed prejudice, keep us trapped where we can't get a fair trial or a change of venue. They spray hate against AIM and Yellow Thunder Camp like drenching the inside of the house with poison gas, and the state and the feds buy the testimony of rotten witnesses like Jones. They have all the power—"

"I know," Eddie interrupted me. Then he grinned. "I know that. They've got everything, but they ain't got us."

17.

One day, Jones was professing love for Collins; and the next day, he was betraying him in the deal he had made with Lefholz. Having been betrayed, Collins might have been expected to react toward Jones with due anger and rage. I knew Collins was fully capable of such feelings. Yet he showed no enmity toward Jones. None. Why not?

None of the physical facts supported the scenario Jones was selling. The coroner's photos revealed the path of a large projectile plowing through Tollefson's muscle and bone, not the kind of ammunition that comes out of a .22. There'd been a struggle in which Tollefson's wristwatch was pulled down into his palm, something that could only have happened on the driver's side of the car, opposite from where Jones said Collins was standing. In addition, the bullet's steep downward course through Tollefson was impossible had Collins shot him from the window ledge on the passenger side of the pickup, or even a little above it. And Tollefson's pistol had been placed in his hand *after* death—by whom was a fact yet to be discovered. And of course, not only was Jones a known killer, but his prior story to the cops about Tollefson shooting himself, a story he'd now abandoned, converted him into a confessed liar.

Then there was Lone Wolf's grand jury testimony, which had placed a story into the record that was contrary to the tale No Heart Jones was peddling.

Again, I asked, why was Collins so comfortable with Jones's apparent betrayal?

What if, I thought, when Jones and Collins were together, Jones manufactured a story that he thought would free them both? Suppose their story went like this: Jones and Tollefson were struggling up there on the ridge above the camp. Tollefson grabbed his pistol and was about to shoot Jones. At that exact moment, Collins arrived on the passenger side of the camper and saw Tollefson's gun come up. At that instant, Tollefson pulled the trigger *and* Collins fired the cut-off .22, killing Tollefson and saving Jones.

A killing to save a third person in mortal danger has been recognized as a valid defense for murder. A stirwise con like Jones would have known that.

I slept on the idea, and the next morning I thought I'd test my latest theory on Collins. We were again sitting in that small concrete-walled box in the jail.

I said, "Collins, I think somebody concocted a plan that was supposed to get both you and Jones off." I outlined my latest theory—that Collins had killed Tollefson to save Jones. Under those conditions, Jones would be safe under his immunity agreement and Collins would have as his defense the killing of one person to save another in mortal danger. I said, "This sounds like something Jones put together."

I searched Collins's face. It was stony, almost embalmed. He stared at me, but his eyes gave me nothing.

"That defense will never sell in South Dakota to an all-white jury," I told him, "especially when the supposed Indian you saved wasn't even an Indian, but a black man pretending to be an Indian."

I could just hear some redneck juror arguing the case: *It's our duty to stop these killings. Are we gonna buy bullshit stories like "I had to kill a white man to save some nigger with a phony Indian name?" It's a white man against one o' them prairie niggers, and a phony one ta boot, one o' them troublemakers from AIM. Weigh 'er up and tell me your decision.*

I was looking straight into Collins's eyes. "In South Dakota, it's all right to kill an Indian to save a white man. But not the other way around."

The muted eyes of Collins Catch the Bear still told me nothing.

I continued: "I think Jones was planted at the camp by the feds. Jones didn't decide to escape from Englewood after thirteen years in the pen with only a month to go. His escape was part of a deal."

Then I asked Collins straight out: "Did Jones figure out this master plan so that both you and he could supposedly get off?"

No response.

I didn't press him. I wasn't ready to press him. But I knew this much: Collins Catch the Bear couldn't have figured out such a plan by himself. He was smart, but his mind didn't work that way.

I put a call in to Lefholz to see if I could catch even a hint as to what was going on. The conversation was friendly, professional, and guarded. I asked him if he knew before Jones signed the immunity agreement how he would testify.

"Of course," Lefholz said. "I sure as hell wouldn't give anybody immunity before I knew what their story was."

"And in exchange for Jones's new story, you gave him immunity?"

"Absolutely. I don't give immunity on credit. He either tells a story that checks out and that we feel is true, or there's no deal," Lefholz laughed to let me know he was still being friendly.

"How about Catch the Bear? How do you expect him to testify?" I asked.

"You going to put him on the stand?"

"Don't know," I said.

"Why would you?" he asked. "He shot that man in cold blood. But I'm always open for your thoughts. We believe in our case, Gerry, and we're ready to go forward with our proof. But if you want to discuss other evidence or other possibilities, I'd be more than willing to do so with either you or Jim Leach."

He was propping open the door for a plea negotiation.

Lefholz was an experienced prosecutor, and he was no wide-eyed novice as a politician. He'd seen strong men finally fold up like pansies in an oven under the terrible heat of a first-degree murder charge. In our justice system, we do not tolerate stretching the accused on the rack until his joints pop free. The law protects us from physical agony, and the Fifth Amendment safeguards us from testifying against ourselves.

But nothing shields us (especially if we're innocent) from being stretched on the psychic rack to endure the torture of a first-degree murder charge. Lefholz, as a seasoned prosecutor, must have known that as the stretching continues and the trial date grows closer, even the bravest begin to disintegrate, seeing the possible horror that awaits: being murdered by the state.

For Collins, the days must have dragged on, minute after endless minute. He must have begged to hear the decision—any decision, please, *any* decision.

Collins Catch the Bear had been confined in that tight concrete-and-steel box for six months. Even those waiting on death row are allowed to exercise. Would Collins break? Would he make a deal, any deal that would release him from the unmitigated pain of the stretching?

I once represented a man charged with murder. The state sought the death penalty with a vengeance. The accused man told me that another inmate on death row had claimed he kept hearing the cawing of a crow in the night, and that he believed the crow was a foretelling of his death. In some cultures, the crow is a symbol of death and its cry a message of death. The man who heard the cry of the crow was found guilty of murder and executed.

The cry of the crow.

The cawing into the night.

The jagged cawing.

I asked my client if he'd heard any crows on death row, and he said no, and he was later acquitted.

I didn't ask Collins if he ever heard the cawing of a crow while waiting to go on trial. I didn't want to know.

The trial was set for March 14, 1983, in Rapid City. An underlying sense of justice kept poking itself into the back reaches of my mind. Did Tollefson get what he deserved, a kind of justice that men understand but the law does not recognize? The white man Tollefson had come to the camp looking for trouble. He knew he was frightening the people below, especially the women and children. He'd likely been experiencing some sort of heady power, some pleasure from his intrusion. He was fully armed, ready for a fight, and he got one. Why kill an innocent Indian kid in retribution?

A lawyer must finally talk to his client about the facts. I looked at the young man sitting across from me on the metal folding chair. I saw how this boy had grown old in six months and as thin and brittle as a dry stick.

I said, "Collins, I've looked into the facts of this case carefully. Nothing in the facts shows you killed Tollefson, and I don't believe you did."

He seemed unimpressed with my conclusion.

I believed Collins was innocent, but I had to hear it from his lips before I could put him on the stand. I spoke to him quietly, looking him straight in the eye. "I talked with Russell Means earlier today. He says he thinks Jones did it. He says he'll smoke the pipe with the men at the camp and find out the facts and let me know."

Collins's face was still empty.

"Collins, if you say you killed Tollefson, I can't put you on the stand to testify that you didn't, because the law says that if a lawyer's client confesses a crime to him, the lawyer can't help the client commit perjury. Do you understand?"

He nodded yes, but I couldn't tell if he understood.

"Let me hear you explain it to me so I'm sure you understand." Another long silence. He looked as if he were going to remain silent. I tried to help him. "Well, let's start this way," I said. "Suppose you did kill Tollefson. Could I put you on the stand to say you didn't?"

"Yeah," Collins said.

"That's what I was afraid of," I said. "You haven't understood me correctly." I went over the ethical double-bind again. This time he answered correctly: no, I couldn't put him on the stand if I knew he'd actually done it. But what if Collins were relying on the supposed defense of having shot Tollefson to save Jones?

"Okay," I said. "Now, if I put you on the stand and you say you *did* shoot Tollefson, but that you shot him to save Jones, the jury will put you in prison forever, even if it's the truth. Do you understand?"

"Yeah," Collins said, looking away.

"Now, look at me! Listen! How many times have you shot a rabbit? Do you think that you wouldn't know the difference if you shot a rabbit with a .357 or a .22?"

"Yeah," Collins said without expression.

"Have you ever shot a rabbit?

"No," he said.

"And Jones's testimony is that you had the end of the rifle resting on the sill of the passenger-side window and that you raised it just a little bit and pulled the trigger. That shot would have made a path nearly straight through and through. The bullet would never have come even close to the vertebrae in Tollefson's neck."

Collins looked away.

"Collins, please. Look at me. Was Tollefson's gun in or out of the holster when he picked it up and swung it around toward Jones?"

He didn't answer.

I knew this young man was highly intelligent. I knew him to be as articulate as a Sunday preacher. His refusal to communicate with me was pushing me toward a decision I didn't want to make: to get the hell out of the case.

"You have to talk to me, or I can't represent you," I said. "Do you understand?"

"I remember the pistol being in the scabbard," Collins said, using the alternate word for "holster."

"Well, that can't be right, Collins! That pistol had three empty cartridges in it. If the gun was fired three times while inside the holster, there'd have been a hell of a lot of powder residue inside the holster, even from just the first shot. Residue would have been impacted into the rough holster leather, no question about that, but the FBI didn't find any residue inside the holster. I have the FBI report in my file, and I've read it carefully. That means the gun wasn't in the holster when it was fired."

"Well, the experts can say what they say," Collins said.

I reached over and touched him lightly on the shoulder. "I think my friend Collins Catch the Bear is taking the rap for some-body, and for something he didn't do, because he loves that camp, loves its spirits, because he finally found his place there, and he thinks he will get off if he takes the rap because he's been told that if he shot Tollefson in the defense of Jones, he can get off. I want you to believe me, Collins. It will not work!"

My entreaty was met with another long silence.

"So, what I need you to do is to trust me. I think I can work out a way so that nobody gets hurt if you'll tell it the way it really was. Maybe you want to think about that overnight. Maybe you'd like to think about all this before you tell me what happened. Would you like that?"

Collins Catch the Bear stared at me like a fighter in the staredown before the bell. I waited.

"Yeah, that sounds good," he finally said. "I'll think about it."

I wanted to hear him say, "I never shot the man." But weird, unpredictable powers can take over the mind of the tormented. In our own small worlds, which are peculiar to each of us, each of us is the judge and jury of the self, and some of us are guilty, guilty or not. Or had Collins simply agreed to an ill-advised strategy concocted by Wambli No Heart?

When I stood up to leave, Collins looked like a small, frightened animal trapped in a cage. Had he acquired the cleverness of one? Or was it I who had outsmarted myself? I left Collins Catch the Bear sitting on his steel folding chair and hollered for the guard.

18.

Eddie, Jim Leach, and I drove up the narrow dirt road through the tall, shady pines of the Black Hills toward the Yellow Thunder Camp. In the late winter, in this place sacred to the Lakota, a place they call the Paha Sapa, the ground was already barren of snow. The small meadows along the road, brown where the grass had cured, had been left untouched by the white man's lazy-eyed cows.

I wanted to see Evans White Face and Smokey White Bull. Jones claimed that those two had flanked him, one on each side, when the bullet ripped through the white man's artery and left life squirting from him like a runaway hose. The sheriff's report said it took a minute to a minute and a half for Tollefson to die.

We bounced along in Jim Leach's old car, which rattled and groaned and swerved too much at the curves, and Jim, skinny as a cornstalk, hugged the wheel, fought it, gave in to it—back and forth over the dust-filled ruts. The rough road jarred our teeth and made our heads bob like agreeing puppets. We met another old car, full of Indians and coming from the direction of the camp, and we took to the shoulder as they sped by with riotous eyes and wide grins on their faces, and we ate their trailing dust on the way to the next sharp curve to the south.

Then the road crossed through another small, brown meadow, one that would have provided winter fodder for the long-gone herds of buffalo. The meadow was empty of all living things except two men shooting their pistols into a target a few yards away. The men were standing by a shiny, new black Chevy van with a psychedelic flame factory-painted in eye-aching colors across its length. Then another old car jammed with Indians again pushed us to the shoulder. This car jumped along, using both sides of the road like a drunken frog. I looked back to see it disappear around a curve. One small, brown-faced child was standing on the rear seat of the car looking back at me with somber eyes.

Jim Leach pulled up in front of the arrow-shaped gate at the Yellow Thunder Camp. A fierce-looking Indian sprang out of the security shack.

"What do ya want?" he asked. He wore loose white man's jeans, a T-shirt, and tennis shoes. A red bandana around his head held back long black hair that fell below his shoulders.

"Looking for Smokey," Jim Leach said in a quiet voice. He gave the Indian a reassuring smile. "We represent Collins Catch the Bear."

"Oh," the fierce Indian said. He lifted up the arrow gate with one long tug of the pulley, and we drove in and parked.

Jim said he knew which tepee was Smokey's, and he went to fetch him. Soon he came walking back with a young Indian whose face was paler even than Collins's. He was of slight build and wore thick aviator-type glasses and a red bandanna folded into a head-band. His long braids, one on each side, bounced to the rhythm of his steps. His legs were bowed and his toes pointed inward.

Jim introduced us, and I suggested to Smokey that we go sit down on the dam in the warm February sun and talk a little, just the two of us. I nodded to Jim. He understood.

This young Indian and I passed the time of day until we were comfortable. Smokey was articulate and seemed open and even trusting, so I finally got to it. I asked him straight out, "Why did you go in and give a statement to the prosecutor, Lefholz?"

"Well," Smokey began slowly, "it was in February. [Sheriff Holloway] and another deputy come out here, and my friend Wolf Slayer let 'em in, and the sheriff wanted me to come in with them. I said, 'Well, I'd like to change my clothes 'cause I'm kinda dirty, and I been doin' a lot of work at the camp,' and he says, 'No, you look clean enough ta me.' An' I was afraid if I didn't cooperate, they might try something, an' for the sake o' all the people 'round here, I thought I'd better go in. Before I went in with them, I asked them if I could call my lawyer."

"Who's your lawyer?" I asked.

"Bruce Ellison," Smokey told them. He continued: "An' on the way in, I asked 'em once more if I could call my lawyer, and they assured me that they would call him. But Bruce Ellison, he never come. Usually you call him and he'll be right over, just like that, in a matter of minutes. But he never come."

We both knew he shouldn't have given a statement to the sheriff's men, much less one on video. But I knew he'd been afraid in the Sheriff's Office, alone and with the sheriff's men surrounding him, so I didn't ask him any more questions about talking to the sheriff, and he fell immediately into talking about the killing of Clarence Tollefson—he must have known that's what I wanted to talk about.

"On the day that the white guy got shot, I was out on the wood run," Smokey said. "And when we come back in the old green truck, we looked over and there he was on the ridge, watching our camp below, and his camper was parked right up there above him. He was lookin' down at our kitchen."

Smokey spoke in easy words uttered in flat, identical sounds. "Collins told us the Tollefson guy was acting mean, and that the guy [Tollefson] told Collins 'not to try it' and stuff. Well, we just waited about five minutes—we thought he'd leave and there wouldn't be no incident. But he just sat there in his pickup, and sat there, and finally we got out o' the truck and went over there and asked him what he wanted. And he started getting forceful," Smokey said.

"What did he say?" I asked.

"He said all kinda things, like 'It's none of your business why I'm here. It's my land, too,' and it went on like that, and pretty soon the guys started running up from the camp below. Wambli was getting obnoxious and loud, and we was still tryin' ta talk ta the guy in a nice way, and then Wambli got in there calling him 'a big man' and saying all kinda things."

"What did Wambli say?"

"Well, when Wambli started scuffling with him, he started calling him a son of a bitch and every other word in the book."

"Scuffling with him?"

"Scuffling."

"Tell me about the scuffle."

"The scuffle got goin' when Tollefson slammed Wambli ag'in the car door."

"Who opened up the car door in the first place?"

"Wambli opened the car door."

"Why did he do that?"

"I don't know. He musta been tryin' ta pull him out o' there or beat him up or somethin'."

"How did he pull Tollefson?"

"By the arm closest to the car door," Smokey said.

"What happened when he was pulling him?"

"Then I saw a .357 Magnum without the holster."

"It came up *without* the holster?" I asked, surprised.

"Yeah."

"And what you're saying is that Wambli was pulling him by the left arm, and Tollefson was coming around with his gun in his right hand?"

"Yeah."

"What happened then?"

"Then is when I heard a few shots go off."

"What did you see?"

"I didn't see anything."

"What did you do?"

"I started runnin'."

"How long was it after you started running before you heard the shots go off?"

"About two minutes."

"Well, now," I said, trying to slow Smokey down, "you mean it was *two* minutes before you heard the *first* shot?"

"Yes. Because I fell down twice while I was running—took me a while to get my senses back."

"You didn't hear any shots at all *before* you ran?"

"No. Right after I turned around, I took about five, maybe six steps, and that's when I heard the shots."

"Well, when I clap my hand, that's when you started to run. Now, I'm going to count. You tell me to stop when you heard the first shot. Are you ready?"

"Yeah."

"One, two, three, four—"

"Stop," Smokey said.

"Right then is when you heard the first shot?"

"Yeah."

"Did you see who shot?"

"No."

"Do you know whether Tollefson shot?"

"No."

"Do you know if Wambli shot?"

"No."

"You know what a .22 sounds like, don't you?" I asked.

"Yes."

"Did the shot sound like it came from a .22?"

"No."

"Why not?"

"Because it was too loud."

"All right. What does a .22 sound like compared to a .357?"

"Popgun," he said.

"What did this shot sound like?"

"Sounded like a shotgun sounds," Smokey said.

"Loud?"

"Yes."

"That's the first shot you heard?"

"Yes."

"Did you turn around to look?"

"No," Smokey said. "I just kept on a runnin'."

"How long was it before you heard something again?"

"It wasn't very long when I heard the popgun shots; that's all I heard."

"Popgun shots?"

"Yes. Right after I heard the big shots—maybe two seconds after."

"What do you think those popgun shots were?"

"I don't know."

"Did those later shots sound like a shotgun?"

"They didn't sound like no shotgun."

"You never turned around to look?"

"No."

"Is it possible that the other shots were from the big gun, too, and that's why there were three shots fired from that gun?" Of course, I was leading.

"Yeah, it might have been, yeah," Smokey said, as if that answered it for him.

"And the reason it sounded like a pop instead of a loud bang was because you were a little farther away, and running?"

"Yeah, that makes sense, don't it?" Smokey said.

"You never saw a .22 up there at the scene?"

"No."

"Did you ever see Catch the Bear with a .22?"

"No."

"In your life."

"Well, I seen him down at the camp afterward with a .22, protectin' the women and children." Then he added, "That first shot about broke my eardrum."

"How far were you from the pickup when you heard that first shot?"

"Well, I ran when I seen the gun in Tollefson's hand coming around, and I musta took four or five steps when I heard the gun go off."

"How long before you heard the second shot?"

"Maybe about four or five seconds."

"How far apart were the last two shots?"

"About a second apart."

"Who did you think was shooting?"

"I thought the Tollefson guy was shootin'."

"Now, to kinda go over this a little to make sure I have it right: Collins went over to talk to Tollefson, who was standing outside his pickup looking down at the camp?"

"Yeah, and when Collins approached, the Tollefson guy, he told Collins, 'Don't try it,' an' Collins come back to our truck, and then is when I seen Tollefson lean down into his pickup and do somethin', and then he got back up again."

"You figure he was getting a gun? Is that what you're suggesting?"

"Loading it up," Smokey said.

"And had Collins made any overt act against Tollefson?"

"No."

"Never took out his knife, started to unsnap it or anything?"

"Didn't do nothing," Smokey said.

"And even though Collins did nothing, Tollefson said, 'Don't try it'?"

"Yes."

"Now, when Tollefson came out with the gun, was it holstered?" I asked again.

"No."

"It was *not?*"

"It was not. He had to take it out of the holster to load it," Smokey said, as if adding proof to his statement.

"I know. But he could have put the gun back in the holster. Did you see the gun when it came around?"

"Yes."

"Saw it when he was swinging the gun toward you?"

"Yes."

"And it wasn't in the holster?" I asked.

"It *wasn't* in the holster," Smokey said finally, once and for all.

But in my file, I had the statement Smokey had given to Deputy Bahr. The file was sitting on my lap as Smokey and I talked. And according to the file, on the day of the shooting, July 21, 1982, at 4:48 p.m., Smokey White Bull said some different things. Bruce Ellison, acting as his attorney, had been with him.

According to the file, Smokey had said that Wambli No Heart, Evans White Face, and he, Smokey, were the only three up there on the ridge with Tollefson. Deputy Bahr asked him, "Who was sitting in the front seat of that old green pickup with you?"

"Wambli," Smokey answered the deputy.

"And Evans was riding in the back with the load of wood?' Bahr asked.

"Yeah."

"Was anybody else around up there?"

"Yeah, this [white] guy was up there, and we asked him to leave. Wambli did most of the talkin'."

"What did you say?" Bahr then asked him.

"Asked him to leave peacefully. Wambli did most of the talking," Smokey said again.

"Did the guy say anything?"

"He said something—I don't know what he said, but he was getting negative about it. We asked him to leave, and he was saying this wasn't our land, and we were saying that this was our land—1868 Fort Laramie Treaty an' all, an' he asked us if we had a deed ta the land ta show him, and he was getting negative, an' we continued ta talk ta him for maybe fifteen, twenty minutes."

In the original statement, Smokey continued: "He was still negative in an unreasonable way, and his eyes, were—well, they would go up, and they'd go back down again, like he was on some kind a drugs or maybe even intoxicated, and we seen the rifle on the dashboard, and we told him that there's no firearms allowed around that area, but he had two of 'em."

"Did he call you names or anything?" Deputy Bahr asked.

"No."

"Did you guys call him any names?" the deputy asked.

"No. We just explained to him about the 1868 treaty and all the rights that we have as American Indians."

"And he reached down?" Bahr asked.

"Yeah, he reached down and pulled a pistol."

"You see a pistol? In the holster?"

"*In the holster*," Smokey said (my emphasis).

"Did Wambli No Heart grab his arm?"

"No. He went like this." [No gesture indicated.]

"Which hand did he hit it away with?" Bahr asked.

"Right hand. I seen Wambli's hand go in."

"You heard the gun go off?"

"Yeah, I heard it go off."

"Just, in succession, right away, as soon as Wambli hit it, it went off? Okay, then what?" Bahr asked.

"Then Wambli ran, and I ran behind that pickup as fast as I could. We all ran together."

"What was said between you?"

"I says—I says, 'Let's get the hell out of here.'"

"How far away were you from the vehicle when you heard the next shot?"

"We were running ahead, maybe ten, fifteen yards—"

"Was there more than one shot?"

"I don't know, just so much confusion."

"How many shots do you think went off?"

"I don't know."

"Two?" Bahr led.

"I don't know."

"Well, for sure you know two," Bahr led again.

"Yes."

"At least two shots," Bahr continued to lead.

"At least two shots," Smokey finally repeated.

"And that's counting the one that went off in the vehicle?" That made the three Bahr was trying to elicit from Smokey.

"Yes."

Smokey had given those answers to Deputy Bahr right after the shooting, and now, as I sat there on the dam of Lake Victoria, I didn't say anything to Smokey—just listened and wondered.

In that same file sitting in my lap were two more statements taken from Smokey, both on February 4, 1983. Bahr and Lefholz had talked to him at length, and after having finally gotten him prepared, they called in the video man.

This time, on the video, Lefholz was asking the questions:

"Now, the first time that Mr. Catch the Bear came from the pickup truck that had the wood in the back of it, did he have a gun?" Lefholz asked.

"I didn't see any," Smokey said.

"Did he come back the second time with a gun?" Lefholz asked.

"No, I didn't see him with a gun then, either."

"Now, you know, Smokey," Lefholz began with a kindly voice, like a father to a child, "that the man didn't shoot himself, don't you?"

"Yeah," Smokey said.

"But at the time of the shooting, you said something to us to the effect that the man did shoot himself, didn't you?"

"I thought he did shoot himself," Smokey said, "'cause of that pistol he was wieldin' at all the people there. I thought that maybe Wambli mighta blocked his arm and the pistol went off or . . .'" He stopped and thought a minute.

"You don't know where Collins Catch the Bear was?" Lefholz said.

"No, I don't recall even seein' him around there. He might be on the other side of the vehicle or—"

"That would be the passenger side?"

"Yeah."

"When did you next see Collins Catch the Bear after the shooting?"

"When he was takin' the women and the children back down to the canyon to the cave."

"About how long after the shooting was that?"

"About ten minutes," Smokey said.

"Could it have been less than that?" Lefholz asked.

"Maybe less."

"Was he carrying anything with him at that time?"

"He had a .22."

"A .22?"

"Yeah, a .22, small caliber, it was a small-caliber weapon. I don't know if it was a .22 or what, but it was maybe a Mini-14 or whatever, I don't know what it was."

"OK, didn't you tell me earlier," Lefholz said, referring to the statement he and Bahr had taken of Smokey just before they put him on video, "that Collins may have carried that rifle in the wood truck?"

"He might a had it in there, but I didn't see it," Smokey said.

"Did you ever see that .22 caliber rifle again?"

"No."

"Did Collins ever tell you anything about the shooting?"

"No, he didn't mention anything. He kinda kept to himself, kinda quiet kind of person."

"Did he ever talk to anybody else about the shooting?"

"No, I don't think so, because I woulda heard something if he told somebody else."

"You don't think he could have told somebody else and you wouldn't have heard about it?"

"That's a possibility," Smokey said.

"Did Collins ever tell anyone that he shot Tollefson to defend against Jones getting hurt?"

"No, I didn't hear anything about that, either."

"Nothing about self-defense?"

"Only thing I thought was that Tollefson shot himself."

"Have you ever heard anybody say that Catch the Bear shot Tollefson in self-defense?"

"Yeah, after they apprehended Catch the Bear, couple months after, somebody was saying it was self-defense."

Lefholz's voice grew animated. "*Who* was saying that?"

"I think I heard it on the radio, it mighta been self-defense," Smokey said.

"Did you hear it from anybody at the camp?" Lefholz pushed once more.

"No."

"Did you ever hear that from Catch the Bear?" he asked one more time.

"No."

Finally, Lefholz changed the subject. "Tell us a little more, Smokey, about this hassle there by Tollefson's pickup truck . . . Did somebody open the door to it?"

"Yeah, Wambli opened the door . . . then a scuffle broke out and I saw that pistol being pulled up from where he had it down here, wherever, and when I saw that I just turned around, and I knew something was gonna happen then, so I just took off. I heard the shots go off and thought they were being aimed in our direction, so we were running as low as we could and trying to keep to the trees."

"How many shots did you hear fired altogether?"

"Three or more."

"Did all those gunshots sound the same?" Lefholz asked.

"I don't recall if they were the same; all I remember was hearing gunshots. I thought they were coming from the same gun—from Tollefson's .357 Magnum."

"How was it that Tollefson tried to close the door to the vehicle?"

"When Wambli started getting obnoxious toward Tollefson, Wambli opened the door and was right up to his face, saying this and that, but I don't recall what he was saying, and Tollefson just reached over and pulled the door shut on Wambli."

"Was Tollefson trying to drive off?" Lefholz asked.

"No."

"Why was he trying to close the door?"

"Probably just to get Wambli out of his face."

"Did you see Tollefson's face at the time?"

"Yeah, his eyeballs kept rolling back up into his head, went back down again every once in a while. That was the only thing unusual."

"Did Tollefson brace his head on his arm?"

"I don't remember anything like that."

"You don't recall Tollefson putting his chin like, say, on his arm or his fist or something?" Lefholz persisted.

"No," Smokey said.

"Did you see Wambli's face?"

"Yes."

"Tell us about that?"

"He was kind of in a rowdy mood because of Tollefson's refusing to leave and trying to cause trouble. So, he was getting more and more obnoxious as Tollefson kept refusing to leave."

"Did you ever hear Catch the Bear say anything?" Lefholz asked, as if Smokey had confirmed for him that Catch the Bear was there all along.

"No."

"Nothing at all?"

"No."

"Could he have said something and you wouldn't have heard it?"

"He might have said something to somebody at some time," Smokey said.

Then Deputy Sheriff Bahr took over.

In court, a witness is protected from marathon questioning by one questioner after another. It's not considered fair treatment—not due process. There are supposed to be no relays, like when a whole pack of coyotes runs after a single jackrabbit until the poor creature is finally exhausted.

Bahr started on Smokey again. "Smokey, going back to the vehicle again, and after shots were fired, did you say that's the first time you saw Collins with a gun?" It was clear that they needed Collins at the scene with a gun in his hand to corroborate Jones's statement.

"No, I didn't see him with a gun there," Smokey said.

"Okay, where was the first time you seen him then?"

"After he was taking the women and children—down there at the kitchen.

"But Collins was there?" Bahr added.

"Yes."

"Was Skip there?"

"Yes."

"Moses there?"

"Yes." Smokey added that Sam and Rudell and Evans and Wambli and Omaha John were all there, too, and Skip was driving the old wood truck, and Smokey was in the passenger side, and Collins was in the back with the wood.

And then Lefholz took over again in the relay, the next coyote after the rabbit. "Smokey, I thought you told us that you thought the rifle belonged to Collins, isn't that right? Did the rifle belong to Collins?"

"Might have been, 'cause I haven't seen it. I never seen anybody carrying that or anything," Smokey said. "We don't allow any kinda firearms inside the camp because of the children.'"

"You don't know where that rifle was kept?"

"No." And the questioning by Bahr and then by Lefholz went on—into the evening.

As I sat at the dam at Victoria Lake talking to Smokey, he told me the following: that Wambli had called Tollefson a son of a bitch and a motherfucker; that Wambli had tugged on Tollefson's left arm, trying to pull him out of the pickup; that the .357 then came around; and that it wasn't in its holster. I remembered the photograph showing Tollefson's wristwatch pulled down into his left palm.

Smokey also told me that day that Evans White Face told him that Wambli carried a sawed-off .22 rifle on his left side, under his shirt and his camouflage jacket. He told me that one time, the sheriff stopped a van full of Yellow Thunder Camp people in Rapid City looking for fugitives and that Wambli was in the van and had that gun on him. The sheriff and the police were there and threw everybody up against the van and searched them well—and that nobody could understand how they had done such a thorough search and hadn't found the sawed-off .22 under Wambli's shirt.

I looked at Smokey White Bull. His was an innocent face: his eyes through his glasses were soft, and the sound of his voice gentle.

At that moment, he turned to me. "Did you ever hear of Crazy Horse?"

"Yeah," I said. "Everybody's heard of Crazy Horse."

Smokey White Bull said, "Well, Crazy Horse was killed by a white man, you know."

"Oh, I said. I didn't know that. Who shot him?"

"Never was shot," Smokey said. "He had too much medicine to get shot. One of the soldiers ran a bayonet through him when he was finally starved out and came in to surrender. And when he was standing there, he saw the Indians in a jail behind bars, and Crazy Horse knew that they would kill him anyway, and he tried to run, and that's when the soldier stuck him in the belly with a bayonet," Smokey White Bull said.

I'd never heard that story.

"Yeah," Smokey said. "And Crazy Horse never talked much, you know. He was a man of visions. He never did make speeches, but after the white soldier ran his bayonet through him, and he was dying, then he made a speech."

"What did he say?" I asked.

"I can't remember," Smokey said. "But Crazy Horse is supposed to come back again."

"Is that right?"

Smokey was looking up to the ridge where Tollefson had been killed. The flagpole stood stiff and stark in the late winter. "Yeah," he said. "Lame Deer had visions, too, you know. And there was a book written about his visions, and Lame Deer claims Crazy Horse will come back as a black man."

"Really?" I said.

"Yeah, that's right. And I think Wambli No Heart read that book about Lame Deer's visions, and he must have got it in his head that he was Crazy Horse, and that he'd come back to retaliate against the whites, and I think he thought he was bulletproof, just like Crazy Horse."

"Why do you say that?" I asked.

"Because when that white guy pulled his gun, I run. I was scared. But Wambli wasn't scared of him."

"Yeah?"

"Yeah, and when Wambli was head of security—you know Russ trusted him enough to make him head of security. Well, he used to write things on the paper there when he give us our jobs, and he would sign the name 'Crazy Horse,' and he wrote things down there that Crazy Horse never said, mostly about war and gettin' guns and standing up for our rights, and he had that militant attitude like Crazy Horse."

I nodded.

"We was tryin' the peaceful approach, and Wambli was tryin' to turn everybody back to the militant approach, like in the seventies, durin' Wounded Knee, and I started to get pissed off at Wambli about his militant way quite a number of times. I never gave up."

I nodded my approval.

"Like I say, we trusted him. Russ Means—he's my father-in-law, you know. Well, Russ, he puts him on as the head of security, and we'd all go in the sweat lodge with him, and we thought he was pretty sincere. When he come here, he said he'd served all his time in the penitentiary, and he said the reason Tollefson got shot up there on the ridge and that no Indians got hurt was because Wambli said he had supernatural powers."

"Like Crazy Horse come to life, I suppose," I said.

Smokey nodded.

Later, when I got back to Jackson Hole, I went to the public library to see if I could find out what Crazy Horse had said in his speech. His last speech was recited in several references in formal black and white, like the tracks of the crow in the snow. He spoke his last words to Agent Jesse M. Lee with a bayonet hole through his belly and dying at the age of thirty-five.

Crazy Horse said:

My friend, I do not blame you for this—had I listened to you, this trouble would not have happened to me. I was not hostile to the white man. We had buffalo for food, and their hides for clothing and for our tepees. We preferred hunting to a life of idleness on the reservation where we were driven against our will. At times we did not get enough to eat, and we were not allowed to leave the reservation to hunt.

We preferred our own way of living. We were no expense to the government. All we wanted was peace and to be left alone. Soldiers were sent out in the winter who destroyed our villages.

Then "Long Hair" [Custer] came in the same way. They say we massacred him, but he would have done the same thing to us had we not defended ourselves and fought to the last. Our first impulse was to escape with our squaws and papooses, but we were so hemmed in that we had to fight.

After that I went up on the Tongue River with a few of my people and lived in peace. But the government would not let me alone. Finally, I came back to the Red Cloud Agency. Yet I was not allowed to remain quiet.

I was tired of fighting. I went to the Spotted Tail Agency and asked that chief and his agent let me live there in peace. I came here with the agent to talk with the big white chief, but was not given a chance. They tried to confine me. I tried to escape, and the soldier ran his bayonet into me. I have spoken.

They said Crazy Horse's father and mother carried his body off and secretly buried him in the hills.

I read the speech to Imaging while she was making breakfast one morning. "That speech makes me sad" was all she said.

"Let me read you what another Indian said: 'What is life? It is the flash of a firefly in the night. It is the breath of a buffalo in the wintertime. It is the little shadow which runs across the grass and loses itself in the sunset.'" I stopped reading and looked up. Imaging's eyes were wet. "These were the last words of the brave warrior Crowfoot as he, too, was dying," I told her.

"Why can't we say words like that?" she said. But I thought her eyes spoke even more eloquently.

19.

Smokey White Bull said he never touched any gun of any kind on the day Clarence Tollefson was killed. He said he never had any weapon in his hand. He said he didn't handle any ammunition. He said he ran before he heard the shot. So, my question to him was legitimate.

"You remember that the Sheriff's Office took a swab from your hands to send into the FBI for testing, don't you?"

"Yeah, I remember," Smokey said.

"How do you explain the fact that the FBI tested the swabs from your hands and from Evans's and Wambli's, and all three of you had barium and antimony in quantities they say is consistent with your having recently fired a gun?"

"What do you mean?" Smokey asked.

"I mean the FBI is going to say it looks like the three of you fired a gun that day."

Smokey shrugged his shoulders. He didn't look upset. Didn't look guilty. "Don't know," he said plainly. "I never touched no gun, and I never fired no gun."

"You're absolutely sure of that?" I asked.

"Yeah," Smokey said. "I'm sure of that."

"Well, somebody's dead wrong, then," I said. "Either the sheriff who took the swabs got them contaminated somewhere or the FBI made an error, or you did."

"Well, I ain't wrong," Smokey said. "I know what I did, and I know what I didn't."

"Well, what about Evans?" I asked.

"He never touched no gun, either," Smokey said.

"Where is Evans? I'd like to talk to him. Is he here?"

"Yeah, he's here," Smokey said, and we started down the road together in the direction of where I thought Evans's tepee must be. "I'll go get him," Smokey said and ran up the steep hillside like a forest animal who feels no difference in its legs when running uphill. Then Smokey and Evans came walking back through the thick pines.

Evans was a slight man as well, no larger than Smokey. He was darker-skinned than Smokey, his eyes were as black as ripe chokecherries, and shining, and he had a shy grin on his thin, bony face. His nose was small, crooked, and his hair was straight to his shoulders. He wore a pair of old running shoes, a dirty forest green plaid shirt, and a pair of Levi's glazed on the thighs where the dirt had worn them shiny.

As the two men came up to me, Smokey said, "This here man is Gerry Spence, and he is workin' as the lawyer for Collins, and he wants to talk to ya."

Evans just grinned back and seemed friendly enough. We walked down the road a piece.

Finally, I broke the silence. "Evans, were you up there before Tollefson was shot?"

"I was in the back with the wood," Evans said in his soft, flat voice.

"That's a surprise," I said. "I thought Collins Catch the Bear was in the back."

"Yeah, he was in the back, too."

We walked on.

"Who was driving?"

"Can't say. Can't remember."

We walked by the security shack. An Indian was hammering away, trying to make a table out of a box and some two-by-fours. Then Evans said, "We asked this guy up there to leave in a nice way, and he gave us some different words."

"When you first came onto Tollefson up there, was Wambli with you yet?"

"Yeah, he was already there."

Why should Evans or any of the others tell the white man the truth? The truth is not in the white man. The truth is too pure for the white man. The truth is more than facts. Facts are not the truth. But the white man wants facts. How far is it to there? The white man writes numbers down, but the numbers cannot see or feel the Mother Earth. The distance to there in the springtime with the yellow bells in bloom is different from the distance to there when the snow is higher than the belly of the moose.

"There was a whole bunch of us up there," Evans said. "There was me and Wambli and Smokey and Catch the Bear and Omaha John and Frank and Danny Spider."

"Rudell?" I asked.

"No. No, Rudell wasn't there." Evans thought for a moment, but the smile stayed on his face as if he figured he'd remain safe as long as it was frozen on his lips. "See, this land is ours," he began. "And this white man said he wanted to see a deed. And then he got really cocky, and Wambli opened the door and hit him on the side of the head, and that's when he reached for his holster, you know, his gun, and it went off, you know." Evans's words came out in quick, small spurts of high sounds, out of the chest, as if spoken through the vocal cords of a boy.

"Now, listen to me carefully," I said slowly, looking squarely into Evans's face. "This is important. You know the difference between the sound of a little .22, a pop, and the sound of a big .357 Magnum, don't you?"

"Yes."

"When you heard the gun go off, the first shot you heard, what did it sound like? Did it sound like a .357 or like a pop?"

"Well, the first I heard was a sound like a high-powered rifle."

"Yeah? In other words, it was a big noise?"

"Yeah."

"Did you hear some other shots after that?"

"Yes. I really can't say. I think about three or four, or two or three—really can't say."

"When I begin counting, that's when you saw Tollefson's pistol coming around. Tell me when it was you heard the shot. One . . . two . . ."

"Stop," Evans said.

"Wambli is there?"

"That's true."

"Where is Collins Catch the Bear?"

"He's running, I think."

"Did Collins have any kind of gun?"

"No kind of weapon. I would have seen it, and I would have told the truth if I did see a weapon, but I didn't see no weapon on him and no kind of gun or nothing.'" He said his words with conviction, through his smile.

"Was there a gun in the camp's old truck?"

"Not that I've known."

"You never saw a gun?"

"No."

"Did you ever see Collins Catch the Bear with a weapon?"

"No."

"And so, the shots went one . . . two . . . first shot, and then three . . . four . . . five—"

"Now!" Evans said.

"That's the second shot, on five?"

"Yeah. And then there was another shot right after."

"Now, you say you saw Tollefson's gun coming up?"

"Yes."

"Was it in or out of the holster when he brought it up from the seat?"

"It was *in* the holster."

"But Smokey said the gun was out of the holster."

"No, it was *in* the holster when he brought it up. In the holster," he said, smiling, but his eyes were not happy.

20.

"I been listenin' pretty close," Eddie Moriarity said to me. "I been talkin' to these guys a little. They can't keep their stories straight. They're coverin' for somebody. But I haven't figured out who yet."

"Well, we'll just keep on listening and see where it takes us," I said.

Evans White Face talked to me like a man telling his story straight and true. He didn't apologize for contradicting his friend Smokey when he insisted that Tollefson's gun was always holstered. He shrugged off that important inconsistency as if it should be expected and understood, as if it didn't matter.

Then I asked, "After Wambli hit Tollefson, what did Wambli do?"

"That was when Tollefson reached for the gun, and Wambli hit at something, and it went off."

"Well, weren't you already running by that time?"

He shook his head in the negative.

"How do you know Wambli knocked the gun up?"

"See, what happened is . . . I'll tell you the truth," he added, as if I finally had him. "When the white man pulled that holster, you know, when he come up with it, well, I ran, and I glanced back like that, and I seen Wambli, and I seen his hand move somehow, and that's when I kept on running, and when I got down here, well, that's when I heard two, three more shots after that, and after ten or fifteen minutes, Wambli come down from up there." Evans pointed up to the ridge where the killing had occurred.

"You think Wambli shot him?" I asked.

"I think he did." He said the words as if the idea satisfied him.

The pathologist had reported, "No evidence of soot, powder residue, stippling, or singeing was evident about the wound." If the pistol was in Tollefson's hand when it discharged, it could have been no more than a few inches from the entry wound, and would have left obvious powder burns around the wound. But if the pistol was still in the holster when it was discharged, there would have been gunshot residue inside the holster. None was reported.

Evans said, "He [Wambli] might have had a weapon on him. I seen him carry one in security before—a .22 sawed-off gun. That's all I can say—that's all I seen."

After I thought I'd asked him everything, Evans then said, "When Wambli hit Tollefson, his eyes kinda rolled back in his head like, and I could see the white part of his eyes."

"*After* Wambli hit him or *before?*"

"*After,*" Evans said.

"Did Wambli jerk Tollefson by the hand with the pistol in it or by the empty hand," I asked.

"The empty hand," Evans said, referring to the left hand, the one nearer the door, the hand with the wristwatch pulled down into the palm, as we saw in the sheriff's photos.

"Did he ever pull him clear out of the car?"

"Not that I seen," Evans said. But Evans had said he was running and glanced back and saw Wambli hitting the man in the face, jerking his left arm. That's all he said he saw.

"Did you guys go back there later and wipe the prints off that gun?" I asked suddenly.

Evans didn't blink. The smile never left his face. "No," he answered as quickly as I'd asked the question.

"Are you sure?" I said sternly.

"Yes, I'm sure. I come back down here after that happened, and I didn't go back up until Russell and Bruce came back up there, and then the sheriff came. I didn't touch nothing," he said. Then he added, "Wambli, he mighta wiped off the prints 'cause he didn't come down for a long time." Then Evans looked at me and broadened his smile a little. "And when Wambli come down, he said that he made the white man kill himself. He said something about the spirit of Crazy Horse."

"And when you got down, Collins was already down?"

"Yeah. I was going to use the bathroom, and a lady was in it." He pointed to the outhouse below us. "And I waited and looked, and Collins was already down at the kitchen, and I was standing right there at the bathroom, and here comes Wambli."

"Did Wambli ever tell you he wiped the prints off that gun?" I asked.

"No. He never said anything." Then he added, "Wambli says he jumped off that cliff, he was so scared." I looked to where Evans was pointing. There were places on the cliff where a man could walk partway down, but about halfway down was a sheer drop-off at least thirty feet above the valley floor.

"Do you know anybody who's ever jumped off that?"

"Nope." Evans said.

"Do you believe Wambli did?"

"I can't see him jumping off that cliff," Evans said, still smiling. "And then Wambli come down here and he says, 'What do you think? I made a white man shoot himself.' He said, 'The spirit of Crazy Horse is here, you know,' and that's what got me, because around here, any talk about spirits—that's a sacred thing. They can come back as lightning, and you can find yourself dead."

"The spirit of Crazy Horse is sacred to you?"

"Yeah, and in the sweat lodge we have our honor seats for the ancestors and the old warriors, and every time Wambli made a list for the work detail, he always signed it 'Spirit of Crazy Horse.' I don't know why. The spirit must be driving him crazy or somethin'."

The sunset felt good as we walked along, but when we got to the brow of the hill below the camp, it seemed time to go back. Eddie and Jim were waiting at the security shack by the car. Jim nodded to us, and Eddie smiled at us through his thick beard.

"We've been talkin' about this Wambli," I said to Eddie. Eddie said nothing back, and the four of us stood there for a moment, waiting for somebody to say something. Evans was smiling down at his feet, and Eddie was watching. A gray pup ran by.

"Wanna dog?" Evans asked.

"I'd like to have one of those pups," Eddie said. I could tell he meant it. Eddie was the kind who wanted every pup he ever saw.

"You can have that pup," Evans said. It was lop-eared and skinny, with a tail as long as its body, rat colored and ugly.

I changed the subject. "We've been talking about [Wambli No Heart] Jones."

Evans picked up on it. "Jones was always pushin' people around at the security meetings and all. Once, he was givin' me hell about some radios which was gone from here, and I didn't know nothin' about 'em, an' he chewed me out for it, so I turned around and I said, 'Just because you're head o' security don't mean you own the whole people here. You don't push people around,' and he said, 'I got the spirit here. I got two spirits at my tepee,' and all that bullshit, you know, and he was tellin' me that he was gonna dance this year at the sun dance."

Evans stopped to gather his thoughts. "I didn't want no part of him, so I just got up and left. I didn't really get along with that Wambli, ya know."

Eddie had also read the transcripts of the sheriff's taped questioning of Wambli. "Which side of the car was Omaha John on?" he now asked Evans.

"On the passenger side—right next to Collins," Evans said. "An' if Collins had a weapon, I woulda seen it real clear. Then I run. Wambli had built a bunker up there on the ridge for when there'd be trouble." We'd seen it earlier—a hole dug down into the loose dirt and rock on the top of the ridge, like a small trench. "And I was runnin' for that bunker, but I tripped over a big rock and missed it, an' I broke my kneecap, and I got up and I started running again. Forgot about the pain, you know." He looked at Eddie, smiling, to see if Eddie believed him.

Eddie asked, "And how did Wambli act when he got back down here?"

"Smart. Real proud like, for having made the white man shoot himself. Said that the spirits made it happen, and Wambli started laughing and said that it could have been us instead of the white man."

"Well, my friend," I said, giving Evans a light slap on the back. "Thank you." I started to leave, but Evans wanted to talk more.

"See, when I started talking in front of Wambli in Lakota, well, he gives me a hex, like I'm talking behind his back, and he looks at me real mean, you know, and he snaps his eyes at me and looks ornery like, but who cares, because I'm not scared o' him. I never told him off, ya know. I never went up to him and said, 'I'm not scared o' you, you know,' because I was waitin' for him— bam! He'd been givin' me a bad time for a long time, orderin' me around,' tryin' ta push me around,' an' I got tired of it, you know, and I was waitin' for him. 'I'll either get ya here in this eight hundred acres or in town or anyplace,' you know, but I never told anybody that. I kept it ta myself."

Then Eddie Moriarity and Jim Leach and I got in Jim's old car, Jim driving and Eddie in the backseat. I looked back at Eddie, who'd always been good at sorting things out, and I said, "Well, Eddie, what's true and what's not true?"

"That's Lefholz's problem to figure out," he said. "These Indians are the state's witnesses, not ours."

"Maybe Lefholz won't call them," I said, "but we need part of their testimony."

"Well, the state has to call them," Leach said.

"Why?" I asked.

"The state can't just call Wambli and not the other witnesses," Leach argued. "They know we'll make a big point about them resting their case on the testimony of an escaped murderer. And if the state calls Smokey and Evans, you can cross-examine them. They can't keep their stories straight, so, we're going to win," he said, as if that settled it.

"No," I said. "If I cross-examine Evans and Smokey, maybe I'll *make* the state's case. It's the state's theory that the Indians are covering for Collins, and Lefholz can argue that the Indians are all a bunch of lying redskins with one objective: to save Collins Catch the Bear."

"Well, that's right," Eddie said, "but if the state puts Evans and Smokey on the stand, they have to explain one thing: all three of 'em, Jones, Evans, and Smokey, had gunpowder residue on their hands. There were three shots fired out of Tollefson's pistol. Is that just a coincidence? Three shots and three men with gunpowder residue on their hands. Maybe Jones killed Tollefson and then Evans and Smokey each fired the gun once in a sort of death pact, so to speak, so they'd all be in it together?"

"Maybe," Jim interjected, as if the idea suddenly interested him.

"And remember," I said, "there's another coincidence. The only three who were supposedly up there at the time of the shooting were somehow related to Means. Smokey is Means's son-in-law, and I'm told Evans is about to marry another one of Means's daughters. And Jones was Means's security chief. All three of these men may have fired a gun, and all three deny it."

I waited for new thoughts to be born. Then I said, "I doubt that poor Tollefson ever fired his gun. He had a bullet through his neck and was only seconds away from bleeding to death. He would have been choking on the blood. When he struggled along the side of his pickup, he must have been concentrating on just keeping on his feet. He fell once, and then he got up and moved toward the back of the pickup, leaning up against it and bleeding out. The sheriff's photos show it. If he ever had the gun in his hand, it would have been covered in blood. Then, in a few seconds, he fell at the back of his pickup and died right there. I doubt Tollefson ever shot that gun," I said.

We drove along silently over the crooked road back to the highway. I was tired and hungry. I wanted to stop for a hamburger, but Leach said we were late for our appointment with Russell Means. He'd be waiting for us in that small, single-story building in town with a sign on the door that read, "Black Hills Alliance."

The building was divided into a few small, poorly furnished offices with a desk and chair here and there. Various posters were tacked to the wall announcing the carryings-on of AIM, and bundles of newspapers put out by the Dakota AIM were stacked on a desk. A white woman with long, frizzy red hair smiled at us as we walked in.

Jim told the woman that Russell was expecting us.

I steeled myself for the man. I could be as tough as he, but I felt tight and tense. Still, I wasn't going to give him a glad hand, a big smile, and a phony how-de-do. We'd look each other in the eye, measure each other up. I'd wait for him to blink and look away, and he'd know I wasn't just some bootlicking white man. If Russell Means was tough, he was going to know he was dealing with his equal.

The woman led us to Means's office, down the hallway. She

knocked and, without waiting for a response, opened the door. Sitting behind an old oak desk was a large Indian who got up with a wide smile on his face. He surprised me. Means stood over six feet tall, every bit as tall as me, and he gave *me* the glad hand and the phony how-de-do. He seemed more like some real estate salesman than a fierce, white man–killing Indian chief.

"Pull up a chair, gents," he said. He motioned us to the straight wooden chairs in front of his desk and let out a little laugh. Yes, a personality-plus man. I couldn't believe it. His complexion was Indian and his face was that of a fighter, even featuring a knifelike scar across the right side of his forehead. His mouth was full-lipped and regular under a straight nose. His hair was parted in the middle with leather-wrapped braids that fell halfway down to his waist. He looked to be in his early forties, with a middle-aged paunch budding at his waist—he probably weighed 220, I thought. I sized him up as men size each other up. All in all, I had to admit: he was a handsome, manly looking man.

Eddie and Jim sat down on a bench in front of the window. I pulled up a chair at the left side of Means's desk. Then he sat down, leaned back in his chair, put his feet up on the desk, and gave me a wide, amused smile.

"Well, boys, what's going on?"

"We've been talking to your people up at the Yellow Thunder Camp," I said. "Trying to find out what happened so we can do a little better job defending Collins Catch the Bear."

"Nice kid, Collins," Means said. "Hell of a nice kid."

"I don't think he killed anybody," I said.

"Of course he didn't," Means said. "That white man killed himself." He laughed. Then he looked serious. "Killed *himself*," he said again. There was no Indian sound to his voice. He spoke precise, well-formed white man's words.

"I was up there talking to Smokey today," I said. "Smokey named the people who were up there when Tollefson was shot."

"Oh," Means said. "I didn't know that." He looked concerned. Then he suddenly laughed again. "Let's see now," he began, as if trying to remember the facts. "Let's see. There were three shots, but only two bullets fired out of the gun. Isn't that right?" He was giving me a false set of facts to test me, to see what I knew.

"No, there were three shots fired out of the gun." I said.

Means put another surprised look on his face.

"Eddie," I said. "Why don't you and Jim step out a minute and see if I can say some things to Russell alone?" It wasn't that I didn't trust my guys. But Means wasn't about to talk with a roomful of white witnesses.

"Sure," Eddie said and left. Leach hesitated a minute and then followed him, a frown on his face.

I pulled my chair up a little closer to Means's desk and began. "Look, Russell, you and I have some things in common. And I understand where you're coming from. If my name were 'Russell Means,' and the whites were beginning to accept my camp, and I was winning the war of public opinion, getting good press and all, and I was also winning in federal court, and suddenly I have a dead white man up there, and the state is claiming my people were involved—well, I sure wouldn't want it to look like any of my folks killed the white man."

I was looking hard into the eyes of Russell Means, who was looking back with a wide, mirthless smile. I continued painting the picture: "That could be the end of what I'd set out to do at the Yellow Thunder Camp. I guess I'd want it to look like an accident, especially if my chief of security, this Wambli, this Jones character, had been the one who killed him."

Means let out a big laugh. "You're funny. All I know is what they told me. And they told me Jones hit Tollefson's arm and Tollefson shot himself. That's all I know."

"Well, things aren't matching up very well, Russell." I took off my hat and set it down on his desk.

"Nice hat," he said. "Where did you get the hat band?"

"Navajo," I said. "Now, Smokey, your son-in-law, told me about Tollefson pulling the gun. Smokey said the gun was *out* of the holster when Tollefson swung on Wambli. But when they found Tollefson, the gun was back *in* the holster. Now, isn't that interesting?"

Means suddenly looked serious. "I didn't know that."

"The FBI said there weren't any prints on the gun. That means somebody wiped the gun after Tollefson was shot and then put the gun back in his hand." I got up from my chair. "Here, Russell. Come over here and sit down. I want to show you something."

With caution creeping onto his face, Means stood, took a couple big steps around to the front of the desk, and sat in the chair next to mine.

"Give me your hand," I said. He extended his right hand. "No, the other one. Now, you're Tollefson sitting in the front seat, behind the steering wheel, okay?" Then I pulled on his left arm at about a right angle to the car body, showing him how I thought Tollefson had been pulled out of the car by his wrist. "This is how his watch was pulled down into the palm of his hand," I said. "Then Tollefson was shot under the ear, and the bullet took a sharp course downward, clipped though the protruding part of his neck bones, and came out his mouth. The killer was probably Jones, who shot poor Tollefson with his own gun. And to make it look like he'd shot himself, the killer wiped the gun and put it back in Tollefson's hand."

"My God," Means said. "That makes sense."

"All you have to see are the pathologist's photos of Tollefson's autopsy. It's very clear that the man was shot with a large-caliber firearm, and I mean a *large*-caliber gun. Tollefson was shot with his own .357. But there's something else. The FBI said there was no gunpowder residue in the holster, so we can prove that the gun was fired three times outside the holster and then was put back in the holster and put in the man's hand."

Means's eyes shifted slightly. "Is that so?" he said.

"Russell," I said, "Jones was a planted snitch."

"Yeah," Means said. "That much I agree with."

"Jones killed Tollefson," I said.

"I think he did," Means said. "I never gave him a thought. I took him at face value."

"Why did you appoint him chief of security?"

"I don't know," Means said. "He just sort of ended up there. He'd been in the joint a long time, and he seemed to know a lot about guns and security and things like that. He seemed like a smart guy. I thought he could help us."

"And you know that when the cops stopped that van in town and searched everybody, Jones supposedly had a sawed-off .22 on him when he was searched, but they claimed they never found it on him. That means to me that he was an undercover snitch in your camp from the beginning."

"Yeah, I'm pretty dumb, aren't I?" Means said, and laughed.

I continued: "And after Tollefson was killed and Jones was printed, Jones didn't run. If he was for real, he'd have known when his prints were sent in that his name would come up as an escaped convict. So, we gotta know Jones stayed there at the camp knowing he was safe from the feds."

"He *was* a snitch," Means said, as if to himself.

Then I said, "Maybe the government's snitch, Jones, ended up killing a government agent, Tollefson. Maybe things were too peaceful at the Yellow Thunder Camp for the FBI. Maybe they needed a little violence. You can't run a bunch of peaceful Indians off their holy land without a good excuse. Maybe what they really needed was some honest-to-god bloody violence at the Yellow Thunder Camp to get the camp shut down."

Means looked like he couldn't find words.

Then I said, "It was Jones who killed Tollefson. It's my opinion—I could be wrong—but maybe Lefholz is using Catch the Bear to get you and Bruce Ellison."

Means reached over and took the telephone receiver off the hook. Then he put a hand over each end of the phone as if he feared it might be bugged.

"And Catch the Bear is innocent," I said.

Means looked at me like a boxer waiting to see where my next punch was coming from.

"I'd like you to go back to your people and find out if somebody didn't actually see Jones kill this man," I said. "Because with all those people from the camp up there when Tollefson was shot, somebody had to have seen something other than that old, stale party line that everybody's put out—that when Tollefson reached for his gun everybody ran and that nobody saw anything; that Tollefson shot himself when Jones bumped his gun up. Somebody had to have seen what actually happened!"

I waited for his answer. After a while, Means leaned over toward me. "I'll go smoke the pipe and find out what the men saw."

"Well, when you find the truth, maybe you should have whoever saw what happened give Lefholz the full story. We'll see what Lefholz does with that information. Lefholz has given Jones immunity. He won't want to put on any evidence in his case that shows that Jones is guilty. But if he knows, if he has credible information that Jones actually did the shooting and he doesn't produce that information for the jury—well, good things may happen."

"Sounds good to me," Means said.

"You may want to know a little bit about who I am," I said. "You don't want to be dealing again with anybody you don't know. Call John Ackerman, the guy who defended you in your murder case. He used to be a student of mine, and he's worked with me on some cases."

"Yeah," he said. "I know who you are. You got that twenty-six million dollars for that Miss Wyoming," he said, referring to the 1980 libel suit brought by my client Kim Pring against *Penthouse* magazine, which I discussed in my book *Trial by Fire*. "So, why don't you put a little of that money in my Indian fund?" He laughed and slapped his leg. Then he took my address and phone number at Jackson Hole. As I was leaving, he motioned to a young pregnant woman walking by in the hallway. "My daughter," he said and nodded to her. She looked mostly white, had light eyes and a pale complexion. "That's Smokey's wife," Russell said.

"Don't be mad at Smokey," I said. "He didn't tell us anything we didn't already know."

Then Jim, Eddie, and I walked across the street to some joint for a hamburger.

21.

On March 16, 1983, Eddie, Jim, and I found ourselves in a courtroom in Aberdeen, South Dakota. Judge Grosshans had provided the prospective jurors in Rapid City with questionnaires, and more than 30 percent had come back with strongly negative comments, such as "I do not know this Catch the Bear person, but if he is one of those AIM Indians he is probably guilty of about anything," and "I think anyone associated with Russell Means is like Russell Means," and "Those Indians at the Yellow Thunder Camp stole it from the National Forest." Judge Ronald Grosshans had reluctantly granted our motion for a change of venue.

Aberdeen is situated in the northeastern part of the state, an old frontier community in Brown County of something like twenty thousand souls. The buildings and Main Street are copies of many such turn-of-the-century western towns. The courthouse is an early twentieth-century stone structure with a tower.

The courtroom was equipped with the usual judge's bench, counsel tables, and a couple dozen rows of wooden church pew–

type benches, uncomfortable public seating that encouraged the audience not to stay too long. We spent six days selecting a jury that Eddie and I thought would be open to our defense.

"Thank God we're in Aberdeen," I said.

"Yeah," Eddie said. "All the comforts of home." We were staying in an eight-dollar-a-night hotel.

Lefholz was making his opening statement to the jury and was coming off like a friendly, honest sort of country lawyer, which I thought he was. Tollefson had been a photographer, Lefholz said. "Just a photographer interested in taking pictures. He had a right to be there in the National Forest."

Lefholz finally got around to telling the jurors that Collins had been on an old wood truck, that he had had a .22 rifle in the truck, and that "this is the gun, of course, that would soon be used by the defendant to kill Mr. Tollefson."

Lefholz told the jurors that a bunch of Indians surrounded Tollefson's camper and hassled the poor man. Then we heard a story we'd never heard before. According to Lefholz, Jones had not been up there on the ridge at the time Tollefson was shot. He wasn't even there! He was down on the valley floor peacefully looking up.

Lefholz told the jury that Tollefson waved down to Jones, who then ran up to the top of the cliff and immediately went to the driver's side of the camper. Lefholz then did what any competent trial lawyer does when his witness is carrying around a life's history that is rotten to the core. He turned to the jurors and in an open, confessing way, said, "Mr. Jones was convicted of murder while in a federal penitentiary in 1971, and since that time he'd been serving his sentence in various federal institutions across the land."

Lefholz then told the jury that Jones was nearing the time of his parole when he suddenly walked away from a minimum-security pen and ended up at the Yellow Thunder Camp. Jones left that minimum-security institution before his time was up, Lefholz said, because the poor man was fearful for his life. Jones was "a peacemaker," Lefholz said. And contrary to all prior testimony from prior witnesses, Lefholz told the jurors that Jones ran up to that ridge to calm things down. It was then that Collins Catch the Bear came around to the passenger side of Tollefson's camper with the .22 rifle. Jones saw Collins with the rifle, and Jones opened the door on the driver's side with the intent of taking over the driver's seat and driving the camper out of danger. But Tollefson panicked, grabbed his .357, and was bringing the pistol up to shoot when Jones reached inside the vehicle and blocked the pistol, because "at that time Jones was fearful for his own life."

Lefholz continued, telling a story I'd never heard from any witness. "Just as the pistol came up and Jones reached out to block it, Catch the Bear said, 'White motherfucker, I'm tired of you fucking with Indians,' and just as he said that, he fired a shot." Those spiteful, foul words Lefholz was now attributing to Collins just before he allegedly pulled the trigger transformed him into an intentional killer with *malice aforethought*, that necessary element for first-degree murder.

And Lefholz provided a new bullet path. He told the jurors, "The bullet itself did not strike any hard object, bone, or tooth . . . so it passed through Mr. Tollefson and in fact came very close to Mr. Jones, who was standing there by Mr. Tollefson."

I remembered the words from the pathologist's report from the autopsy, which showed that "the wound track extends anteriorly downward, and to the left[,] passing through the musculature of the base of the skull and then through the transverse processes of C2-3," the protruding bony horns on either side of the vertebrae.

I was hearing more new information in the case: Lefholz accounted for the three fired cartridge cases found in Tollefson's .357 by claiming that Tollefson had fired his own gun. "He [Tollefson] staggered out of the vehicle and he fired some shots, one shot or three shots. The evidence is not going to be entirely clear on that. One of the bullets just randomly went into the Tollefson vehicle."

Lefholz told the jury that Jones had lied previously when he said he'd blocked Tollefson's gun and that it discharged, killing Tollefson. Lefholz said, "He [Jones] gave this evidence because he was scared—he was afraid of retribution from the camp, of other camp members who had told the same story, so he, too, wanted to tell the story. He also was afraid of being detected. He knew he was an escapee, and he knew he shouldn't have left the federal penitentiary in Englewood."

What we had at this point was Jones, a convicted murderer and confessed liar, standing as Lefholz's star witness under an immunity agreement that would save him from further prosecution in both state and federal court, including the crimes of escape and murder.

Then Lefholz dealt with a couple more problems: the hands of Smokey, Evans, and Jones were all tested for gunshot residue, and all three tests came back positive. He provided no explanation for that finding by the FBI.

And one other problem: As we've seen, the bullet path though Tollefson, as revealed by the autopsy, was a large, ugly wound with a diameter several times the size of a bullet from a .22. But Lefholz told the jury, "The forensic pathologist is not going to be able to tell you exactly what kind of firearm did this. He [the pathologist] will be able, at least, to rule out the fact that it was not a high-powered rifle that shot Tollefson," whatever that meant. Then came what I thought was the last straw. Lefholz referred to Collins's loving letter to his sister, the one we'd already seen, which ended:

> My trial should be around the middle of January. My sights for it are neither high nor are they the lowest, real hard to say at the moment. Real glad you thought to

write. You lifted my spirits a good deal. I'll close now so kiss your little one for his (bad guy) uncle and best wishes to Stan. I wish you a lot of health and happiness with your family and my respect comes along with it.

Take good care.

Collins

Here is what Lefholz said about this letter: "The evidence will show that he [Collins] had a chance, talking to his sister, to deny that he had committed this crime and did not do that."

Eddie Moriarity was on his feet and to the bench. Quietly, he moved that Judge Grosshans declare a mistrial. He protested: "What Prosecutor Lefholz has just done is to blatantly violate Collins's Fifth Amendment rights, the right to remain silent, and he is saying because Collins Catch the Bear, who expressed misgivings over the trial, did not say to his sister that he *denied* the murder, therefore he must be guilty . . . I say it's not only a violation of Collins Catch the Bear's Fifth Amendment rights. It's a blatant, intentional, deliberate violation in bad faith and not only justifies a mistrial; it justifies a dismissal of the entire charges against Collins Catch the Bear."

Then I piled on: "And what if I said in your court that Collins Catch the Bear wrote seventeen letters to seventeen different people and said, 'I didn't kill Mr. Tollefson, and I wanted to introduce those letters to prove his innocence, you would say, 'Mr. Spence, you know better than that.' After we've all worked so hard to see that Collins gets a fair trial, for Mr. Lefholz to wait until the middle of his opening statement to get up and say that this young man is guilty because he didn't deny his guilt when he wrote his letter to his sister is the most reprehensible thing I've ever heard in a courtroom in thirty years from a prosecutor with long experience, and I think we're entitled to have this case dismissed."

Lefholz interrupted my argument. "We've researched the question, and our legal position is standard in the law. It's called 'a missed opportunity to deny guilt.'"

Grosshans seemed astounded: "'Missed opportunity to deny guilt'?" He then asked for the prosecutor's research. "Get me those cases," he said, and adjourned the trial until the following morning.

The next morning, the prosecutors arrived armed with Supreme Court justice Sandra Day O'Connor's words. She had written that "The values behind the Fifth Amendment are not hindered when the state offers a suspect the choice of submitting to the blood alcohol test or having his refusal used against him."

Lefholz asked how this was different from demanding that the accused deny his guilt or from using against him his failure to do so? He argued that even if the state was wrong in having used Collins's letter against him, there had to be an actual showing of jury prejudice to justify the granting of a mistrial, "and even assuming that some prejudice was created, I submit, Your Honor," Lefholz argued, "that the prejudice is so completely buried and reduced to insignificance that it would be like looking for the tip of a needle in a haystack."

Judge Grosshans wanted to know what witness other than Collins could explain what he'd written in his letter. He waited for an answer from the prosecutors. Finally, he answered his own question: "There's no one who can explain what was going though Catch the Bear's mind when he wrote the letter to his sister except the defendant, Catch the Bear himself." So, the prosecutor's use of this innocuous letter to argue that Collins had "failed to deny his guilt" violated Collins's Fifth Amendment right against self-incrimination.

And how did Collins's letter to his sister get into the hands of the prosecutors? I offered to prove how. "These are young girls, ages eighteen, sixteen, and fourteen. These young girls were told that letters were being gathered up to be used for the benefit of Collins. They will so testify, and they gladly gave them to the officers with that representation. Now the question arises," I said, "why did these officers want these letters?

"It suggests to me that from the beginning, Mr. Lefholz planned this kind of attack on Collins in a case where they really have no case except for the testimony of Jones . . . and to force Collins to take the stand to explain his silence is a gross violation of the basic constitutional rights of an American citizen."

The judge was making notes as I spoke.

I continued: "Why did the prosecution do this? Well, one thing is pretty obvious. Mr. Lefholz is a politician. He's sitting down there in Rapid City, and he'd like to close that Yellow Thunder Camp. He's made a desperate agreement with a criminal, Mr. Jones. There were fifteen witnesses out there, and there isn't a single one who will stand up and say that Collins Catch the Bear pulled the trigger."

I turned to Lefholz's argument about the gunshot residue on the hands of the three Indians chosen by Russell Mean to speak to the authorities. "All three had gunshot residue on their hands," I said, "There is only one way that those three people could have barium and antimony in quantities sufficient to be consistent with firing a gun, and that is the probability that all three were involved in the death of Tollefson. There happens to be three shots gone from that gun."

I stopped to catch my breath.

"And remember," I said, "the officers sacked up the hands of Tollefson to test them for gunshot residue, and for some reason they never tested his hands, and yet they tell the jury that he shot his own gun. But his hands were never tested. Why?"

Maybe Lefholz had ended up with jurors he didn't want—an Indian foster brother was on the jury along with a first alternate juror who was a quarter Indian. Was he trying to get the judge to declare a mistrial so that the case could be tried later with a different judge and a different jury?

I began to reflect aloud. Why was I in this pro bono case in the first place? I told the judge how Jim Leach had called me and presented me with a compelling case of Collins's innocence. Leach had told me how Lefholz had offered a convicted, escaped murderer immunity from both murder and escape, offered to get him paroled, and gave him a new identity in exchange for his statement that Collins Catch the Bear had killed Tollefson.

"I don't know what my function is in this world, Your Honor," I said. "I just know that I try to do those things that I feel I should do, and I felt like I should be in this case. That was the answer I gave Collins, and that is the answer I give you, Your Honor."

I told the judge that I saw Collins as a potential leader of his people. "He is a very deep-thinking person, caring and sensitive. He has a great commitment to his people, and those of us who know him believe there's an obligation on our part to preserve the potential leaders of the Lakota people. I would like to see this young man as a mature man leading his people."

Then I wondered aloud to His Honor what would happen if the case were declared a mistrial but "not with prejudice," meaning that the state could start the case anew with another jury and perhaps another judge. Would I be able to come back to defend Collins again?

I said, "I will tell you something, Judge. I've not been to my office for over a month and a half. I haven't seen a client. I haven't taken a deposition. I haven't written a letter. I've been totally engaged in this case one hundred percent of the time. Ed Moriarity has been here solidly for the last two weeks. Jim Leach has been involved here for three or four months, doing nothing but this case. It has been a huge financial hardship on us. The cost of this case is running into five figures out-of-pocket costs to us already. I am not beating my chest. I've taken this case because I wanted to do it. I feel good about taking this case, but it's a luxury, and you can only give yourself so much luxury. Pretty soon you have to pay your employees and the bank, and I think Mr. Lefholz knows that."

I told the judge that I believed that when Lefholz made his statement about Collins's letter to his sister, he *wanted* us to move for a mistrial. We had to move for one, or we would be considered as waiving the error—that is, allowing it to stand—and that would be grounds to charge us with ineffective assistance of counsel. I said that after all the effort the judge had gone to to see that Collins got a fair trial, it must make him sad, yes, it must hurt him to see what had happened.

"I believe that you know there isn't anything you can really do to correct this wrong. I think you know that if you grant a mistrial, that it really could hurt us more than help us, unless you make it with prejudice, so that these charges could never again be brought against Collins. So, Your Honor is on the horns of a dilemma—if you don't grant a mistrial, Collins is hurt; if you do grant a mistrial without prejudice, he is hurt worse. Where does that leave us?"

I pointed out that the judge had invested his life and career in the Rapid City community; his family was there, and that is where he'd chosen to live his life. I said, "You have to go home to a place where people are raging about the Yellow Thunder Camp, and they expect [the camp] to be closed and expect this case to be used for that purpose. It takes a lot of courage to do what the record requires you to do, and I don't think it's right that the onus of having 'turned Collins Catch the Bear loose' should be on Your Honor. It should be on the shoulders of the prosecutor."

I said, "It angers me that this has happened to you. I guess sometimes judges have to make hard decisions. I can say that, but it doesn't tell you how I really feel about it. I feel bad that somebody who is not responsible for any of this may ultimately have to take the blame for this dismissal. That hurts me, Your Honor. I don't think it's right. I think Mr. Lefholz should come forward to

Your Honor and say, 'I am going to dismiss this case myself before you rule.'"

It was Lefholz's chance to respond. "That is a preposterous argument that defense counsel has made—that I would try in any way to remove this court from this case." He then pointed out that he had tried other cases before this same judge and had never attempted to remove him. He said he could have gotten a different judge on the case, "and to say in any way that I am not satisfied with this court trying this case is just absolutely preposterous." He said he would never criticize the court publicly. "There are a number of other points, of course, that Mr. Spence talked about, and as far as trying to dignify any of those with a response, I choose not to do that at this time."

Judge Grosshans's face carried the message of an unhappy man committed to do painful work. He was about to deliver his opinion.

22.

We lawyers were gathered in Judge Roland Grosshans's chambers. I could see he was fighting against threatening tears. But tears for whom? Although they were of opposite political faiths—Lefholz, a Democrat, and the judge, a Republican—the judge had been fond of Lefholz, having even gone so far as to encourage him to run for higher office.

Perhaps the judge was about to castigate Lefholz as a father might express disappointment in an errant son. But would he kick his son out of the house? Would the judge throw the case out and turn Collins loose? In America, we like to talk a lot about the rights of citizens no matter how powerless they are. We proclaim that the poor, the pathetic, and the powerless will receive the same protection under the law as the rich, the ruthless, and the remorseless. With pride, we preach such principles to our children—only to discover that in real life, power nearly always prevails.

My eyes were glued to Judge Grosshans as he struggled to begin his decision. Was he hearing a voice that said, "Listen, Judge, you are about to cut your own throat by ruling for this Indian"? After all, the first rule of human conduct is self-preservation.

But our judicial system, as burdened as it is with incompetence and politics, occasionally produces judges so deeply committed to justice that they will put their own political future in jeopardy. Was such a noble commitment to justice at work here in Judge Grosshans? In South Dakota, judges are elected by popular vote.

My heart was pounding, my breath coming short, my jaw clenched, my eyes fearfully pasted on His Honor. These are the terrifying moments in a trial lawyer's life, moments when we wait for another human being over whom we exercises no control to decide the fate of our client. In a few seconds, words would fall from the lips of the judge and forever change Collins Catch the Bear's life, and ours.

Grosshans began by warning us that his decision was going to be harsh. "Mr. Spence was right in one respect—although I knew it when I took this job four years ago—there would be times when I would be called upon to make a tough decision . . . and now it brings me close to tears, and I guess that's about the best thing I can say."

Lefholz, fearful of where the judge might be going, interrupted him. "I urge the court not to dismiss this case with prejudice, because if you do, you're precluding us from ever coming back again with this case." Yes, and Collins would be free of those charges forever—and of course, the judge's decision could affect both his and Lefholz's political careers.

The judge turned to Lefholz. "I always have had a great deal of respect for you, Rod. In fact, I don't know whether you know that or not; maybe I never said it directly." Then the judge called the jury back into the courtroom to hear his decision.

Judge Grosshans explained to the jury the meaning of the Fifth Amendment of our Constitution—that a citizen was protected from testifying against himself. Then he called the jury's attention to Lefholz's opening statement, when he told the jury that Collins had a duty to deny killing Tollefson in the letter he wrote to his sister, and that his failure to do so was as good as an admission that he had killed the man. The judge said that the statement by Lefholz to the jury had violated Collins's Fifth Amendment right against self-incrimination.

Lefholz had argued that he was merely proceeding under what he called the doctrine of "missed opportunity to deny." But, the judge said, "I've never heard of such a doctrine." He read to the jury Collins's letter to his sister. Then he said, "The State has taken a totally innocuous letter from the defendant to his sister and turned it into a sword against the defendant—not by what the letter said, but by what the letter did not say. The system is geared to assure one charged with a crime that his silence will not be used against him, and I believe a person is entitled to rely on those assurances."

The judge continued: "Suppose the defendant during these past eight months and while in custody had come in contact with five hundred different individuals. Must he in all cases say to each, "I deny doing it," and if he misses one or more, can it be used against him as a 'missed opportunity to deny'? . . . And how could the defendant explain himself without taking the witness stand?" the judge asked. That, of course, would force Collins to give up his Fifth Amendment right protecting him from testifying against himself.

It was now clear to us that the judge was ruling that the prosecutor had violated the court's order. What was not clear was whether Grosshans would merely give Lefholz a slap on the wrist and allow him to start the case over with a different jury, or take the terminal step and throw the case out *with prejudice*—that is, free Collins permanently of this murder charge. The judge's decision would turn on whether he found that Lefholz had committed this wrong "knowingly and intentionally."

Then, still speaking aloud, the judge began a conversation with himself: "Now, what must be done? Obviously, what was said was improper. Can I salvage this case by admonishing the jury to disregard the comment of Mr. Lefholz? To do so, I would have to repeat his comment so that the jurors would know for certain what to disregard. This might tend to emphasize the improper comment.

"How do I 'unring the bell,' a legal aphorism often in use by lawyers and judges that asks how do you erase from the ears what the ears have already heard?"

The judge then spoke about Lefholz's threats to Jones at Jones's deposition. "I found that Mr. Jones's testimony on one occasion during the deposition had been prompted and corrected on a material point by his own attorney, and that was improper. Further, that the comments by Mr. Lefholz to the state's primary witness, Mr. Jones, during a recess, could be construed as a threat. The defense attorney [Eddie Moriarity] alleged the comment was as follows: 'Mr. Jones, the story that you told us first was represented to us as being the truth. You should be advised that if you change that story and have lied to us you will be prosecuted for murder.'"

Judge Grosshans then said, "I found that Mr. Lefholz was negligent in making the comment he did to Mr. Jones and reprimanded him."

The judge also remembered that Lefholz had tried to systematically exclude Native Americans from the jury, saying, "The State must keep in mind that a prosecutor's duty is not simply to convict, but to do justice."

But was the judge going to dismiss the case permanently or was he simply going to order a new trial with a new jury and possibly a new judge? If the latter was the judge's decision, we had outsmarted ourselves. Lefholz would get what he must have sorely wanted, a new judge and a new jury, and as for us, could we afford to represent Collins again?

Then we heard Judge Grosshans proclaim, "It is well settled that jeopardy attaches when the jury is empaneled and sworn to try the case. Needless to say, this jury has been empaneled and they have taken the oath. Jeopardy has attached"—which, in laymen's terms, simply meant that if the judge dismissed the case, it could not be retried, and Collins would go free.

The judge cited a U.S. Supreme Court case that held that when the error was motivated by the bad faith, gross negligence, or overreaching by the prosecutor, where the mistrial was intentional, the state would be precluded from retrying the case. However, the Court also said, "It must be shown that there is actual prejudice or intent to harass, inferable from the fact of actual harm to the defendant."

Judge Grosshans was being careful. He said that in light of that U.S. Supreme Court case, he was required to make some findings of fact. He said that Lefholz was a good man for whom he had respect, and he did not want to be needlessly cruel to him; he respected him. He continued, saying that as the prosecutor, Lefholz "had erred as humans do. However, has the defendant been prejudiced if he is retried?" Grosshans asked. "Without a doubt," he said, answering his own question. "He will have to marshal his defenses again. He is indigent. He has benefited from the intense work of three lawyers, Mr. Spence, Mr. Moriarity, and Mr. Leach, who have given their services to him without compensation. It is not reasonable to expect that they can continue to do this for the defendant forever. Next time, he may not be able to have such representation, certainly not for free. So, yes, he has suffered prejudice," the judge said.

He continued: "Also the defendant must go through the mental strain of again waiting months for a new trial in another locale . . . I do believe Mr. Lefholz's comment constituted gross negligence."

Then the judge tried to make his decision airtight and waterproof. "So, in light of all the circumstances, it is my finding that the mistrial was a result of gross negligence and overreaching by the prosecution, which resulted in actual prejudice to the defendant. The prejudice is such that the defendant would be unable to obtain a fair trial in the future. *Therefore, the case is dismissed with prejudice.*"

Collins was free forever of the murder charge. We had won his case.

Judge Grosshans gave these brave parting words to the jury: "If our Constitution and our laws mean anything other than mere words that we give lip service to, as is the case in other countries such as Russia and [in] Central America, they must be given true meaning here. I believe that this is the best I can do."

Judge Grosshans then banged his gavel to announce the end of the hearing, thanked the jury for their service, and left the bench.

I looked over at Eddie and Jim. They were silent. Then Eddie grabbed me and hugged me. Jim had a small, distant smile on his face. I looked at Collins.

"We won, Collins," I said.

He didn't answer. His face was as expressionless as stone.

While Collins was awaiting trial on this murder case, he'd been resentenced for walking away from the Friendship House five weeks early to join his tribesmen at Yellow Thunder Camp. He was given a maximum of five more years by the federal judge and shipped back to the federal pen in Englewood, Colorado, to serve his sentence.

In the meantime, the state appealed Judge Grosshans's dismissal of the murder case with prejudice. In its opinion of June 6, 1984, the Supreme Court of South Dakota announced that "the sole issue on appeal is whether the trial court [Judge Grosshans] erred in finding that the state's attorney intended to provoke the mistrial motion." Following is what the state supreme court said:

The State readily admits that the comments made during the opening statement were an improper infringement upon Catch the Bear's constitutional right against self-incrimination. Nevertheless, the State maintains that the record in the case fails to substantiate the trial court's finding of intentional misconduct . . . Since the trial court made a specific finding that the State's attorney provoked the mistrial motion, this court must make a determination that the trial court's findings are clearly erroneous before the court's order can be reversed.

The South Dakota Supreme Court said that Judge Grosshans first described Lefholz's conduct as *negligent.* That wasn't enough. It had to be *gross negligence* or *intentional.* The court said that this sequence of findings (from negligent to gross negligence) showed that Judge Grosshans's first feelings were that the prosecutor was merely negligent. The court then agreed that the prosecutor's argument about the so-called "missed opportunity to deny guilt" had no merit, but that "the State's attorney actually seemed to believe in their validity." The state supreme court then pointed to Lefholz's statement to the judge that he had acted in good faith and had not intentionally committed misconduct himself.

Jim Leach argued for our side. He pointed out to the state supreme court judges that at the time of the trial, Lefholz had been running for attorney general, that Jones had been accused of altering his testimony, and that Lefholz's case was crumbling, and its loss would have hurt him politically.

The court countered, remarking that it was "hard to believe the state's case was absolutely futile, and as a politician it would have been counterproductive for Lefholz to provoke a mistrial based on his lack of knowledge of the law."

Jim then argued that Lefholz's statement was intentional because he made it within an hour of the judge's telling him not to. But the high court held that there wasn't enough evidence of intentional misconduct to sustain the judge's dismissal of the case with prejudice. For these judges, enough was not enough.

They didn't approve of what Lefholz had done, but they held that a mistrial with prejudice "was an inappropriate manner of punishing a negligent state's attorney." They never said what an appropriate punishment for Lefholz might be. And I didn't know that punishment of the state's attorney was the issue. I thought the case was about one small, powerless Indian named Collins Catch the Bear, and the issue was his right to a fair trial.

Now Collins would suffer more. Lord knows who would be representing him. Talk about punishment: another trial for Collins and months more waiting for a trial date, and after that, another trial. I wondered if Collins could endure further torture. An accused who is as innocent as a snowflake can survive only so much heat.

23.

Our continued defense of Collins in his approaching murder trial would put our small office to the test. I felt as if the court system, using time as its accomplice, was stretching us on some medieval torture rack. We had other clients whose demands for justice were as desperate as Collins's. If we fled from this battlefield, we would be defeated, not by justice, but by our inability to stay the course in a judicial system bogged down in its own quagmire of politics and precedent. We had no choice, and I still thought a victory in our defense of Collins was preordained. Only a delay, only the indomitable power of time could wear us away and at last defeat us. Once again, we began preparing our defense.

One can defend a client in a criminal case only by attacking. It is the art of war. It is the strategy of every champion in the ring. If one only defends, one loses. For the second trial of Collins Catch the Bear, I had planned a defense that would hoist Prosecutor Rodney Lefholz, along with his witness Wambli No Heart Jones, by twin petards and require Lefholz to defend both. How could Lefholz embrace a convicted murderer and a confessed liar in order to convict one small, skinny, frightened Indian boy? I had Jones's criminal record in our files.

Any cross-examination of Jones would strike at the heart of the state's case. Some of my questions on cross-examination would sound like this:

"You are an escaped convict, Mr. Jones, isn't that true?"

"You've led a life of crime since the age of nine when you knifed your nineteen-year-old cousin, isn't that true?"

"And in 1969, at eighteen, you robbed a soldier and you were sent to federal prison, isn't that true?"

"A year later, still in prison, you stabbed to death a fellow prisoner in the heart and were convicted of murder and sentenced to life in prison, isn't that also true?"

"Murder was old hat for you. You murdered Clarence Tollefson there above the Yellow Thunder Camp, isn't that true?"

Who would believe his denial?

I'd question him on his life as a snitch. He'd habitually served himself by turning on fellow prisoners with his lies, in return for which he earned transfers from Leavenworth to "easier" federal prisons like Lompoc in California and Englewood in Colorado.

On March 26, 1982, No Heart Jones walked away from a work detail at Englewood and arrived at the Yellow Thunder Camp. Within a few weeks, he had so impressed Russell Means that Means made him his chief of security. He became second in command only to Means, a testament to Jones's talent as a fake and a fraud. If a prosecutor was searching for a snitch with a proven record as an expert liar, few could compare to James Lee Jones Jr. Even Jones's claim that his mother was Indian was a lie. Indeed, his official birth certificate declared that he was born on October 25, 1950, in Fayetteville, North Carolina, and that his mother was Jessie Williams, whose race was stated to be "Negro." At the time of his escape from the Englewood penitentiary in 1982, where he had been serving a life sentence for second-degree murder, he was holding himself out as being an Indian known as "Sitting Eagle."

Lefholz must have known his witness was not only a murderer, but a professional liar. Yet Lefholz had given this murdering liar, this escaped convict, his freedom and immunity from prosecution in exchange for his testimony against Collins Catch the Bear. For a bargain like that, I was sure that Sitting Eagle, or Wambli No Heart, or James Lee Jones Jr., or whoever else he claimed to be, would testify to whatever set of facts were presented to him.

My cross-examination of Jones would take Jones into deeper waters: I'd review his statements to each of the other witnesses at the scene, revealing how he claimed that he and Tollefson had struggled for the gun and that Tollefson was shot by his own gun in the struggle. I saw no way for Jones to prevent being pegged not only as an inveterate liar, but also as the sole killer of Clarence Tollefson.

The statements of the Indian witnesses, both under oath and otherwise, provided a hopeless entanglement of fictions, inconsistencies, and speculations concerning the carryings-on above the camp with the white man. Truth was crying to be heard, but where was it hiding? It was concealed in the mutual disdain and distrust between whites and Indians.

The cross-examination of Jones would tell the final story:

"Then you made a deal with Mr. Lefholz. And in exchange for a different story than the one you'd already told to the police, he offered you freedom from your life sentence as a convicted murderer, isn't that true?"

"And your new story was that Collins Catch the Bear, not you, was the killer?"

I'd told Collins we could beat the charges and win his case. I had little doubt of that. Jim Leach agreed, and told Collins we could win the case for him.

Then, suddenly, Collins changed his mind and told me he wanted to plead guilty to the first-degree murder of Clarence Tollefson.

What insanity was motivating him?

Such a plea would result in a life sentence in the pen. It sounded like a death wish, a kind of stir-crazy insanity.

Was Collins suffering from a martyr complex, elevating the needs of all others above his own? Was he a man who would suffer—yes, even die for—the sake of his people and thus bestow meaning on his own life?

All along I'd been arguing that Collins had spent his life compulsively searching for his *place*, and that he'd finally found it at Yellow Thunder Camp. There, at last, he belonged. Perhaps he saw that when Clarence Tollefson was killed, this sacred place was threatened. And one might mix into Collins's emotional cauldron his apparent caring for Wambli No Heart Jones. Finally, add in Collins's sense of his own worthlessness. Perhaps he saw martyring himself as a rare opportunity to give meaning to an otherwise meaningless life. He could save the people at the camp. He could save the camp itself. And his love for *place* was so consuming that he was willing to give up his life for it. In the end, he could be remembered as a true Lakota, like Red Cloud and Crazy Horse and Sitting Bull, who gave their lives for their people and their *place*.

I thought that Collins's love for Yellow Thunder Camp was a foreign force that had captured the case. Science does not deal in love as a reliable diagnostic measurement for understanding the actions of our species. Love cannot be quantified. It may be here today and gone tomorrow. It can be everything and nothing. It can disappear with a word. Indeed, some scientists who claim to know have declared love itself as a form of insanity.

How could I permit Collins to plead guilty to a murder I felt certain he hadn't committed? I'd demand that the court order a mental examination of him before I'd allow such a perversion to consume him. I'd argue into Collins's face until he wilted. I'd never permit such a suicidal act on my watch, and I thought that Collins knew I'd block his choice of death over life.

Then he fired me.

Jim Leach was astounded. "Why did you fire Gerry Spence, Collins? He's your best hope for an acquittal. Don't you want your freedom?"

Collins said, "I just don't want him."

Leach said, "What about Eddie Moriarity?"

Collins said, "I don't want him, either."

Leach asked, "Why, Collins?"

Collins said, "I just don't want 'em."

Leach said, "Collins, you know if we lose, it's your life, in prison."

Collins said, "Yeah, I understand. But I think you can handle it."

Leach said, "But Collins, with me you stand a chance of being convicted, and you don't stand that same chance with Gerry."

Collins said, "I understand."

Leach asked, "How about Evelyn?" He was referring to Evelyn Lifsey, our investigator. Jim thought her help would continue to be valuable.

Collins said, "I don't like her always coming around, and I told her to stop coming around."

Leach said, "Then I'll have to find some others to help me work on the case, and I don't want you vetoing them, too."

Collins said, "That depends on who they are. It is important to me who works on my case."

Jim told me later, "I wanted to be firm with Collins but not too firm. I didn't want to risk losing him. It was essential to my own effective handling of the case that I put some emotional distance between myself and the final outcome. I couldn't put the whole case on my shoulders and expect to retain my sanity and effectiveness. And I had to keep Collins protected from himself."

Collins's trial on the charge of first-degree murder had been set for March 5, 1985, in Sioux Falls, the county seat in Minnehaha County,

South Dakota. On Leach's motion, the venue had been changed to Sioux Falls by Judge Grosshans. On February 19, 1985, a few weeks before the trial, the State of South Dakota, on the one hand, and Jim Leach, along with his new co-counsel, Jeff Viken, on the other, advised Judge Grosshans that a plea agreement had been reached.

They'd all gathered in the county courthouse in Rapid City before a planned trek to Sioux Falls for the trial. Lefholz had been defeated in his run for attorney general, and by then, Dennis Groff was the state's attorney for Pennington County.

Jim Leach reported to Judge Grosshans that the parties had agreed to a plea of second-degree manslaughter with credit for time served.

Judge Grosshans responded to Leach: "The Court requires a factual basis for the plea, and I am going to insist that it come from your client, Mr. Leach."

"I understand that, Your Honor," Leach replied.

From reading the transcript of those proceedings, I thought the good judge had grave doubts that Collins was guilty.

Years later, I asked Jim Leach, "What was motivating Collins to plead guilty to anything, much less to first-degree murder?"

Leach replied, "Who knows about motivation? Mental illness? Guilt?"

I asked him, "How were you able to convince Collins to plead to something less than first-degree murder?"

"I don't know," he said. "Maybe rationality broke through. I am not trying to be flippant. I am just acknowledging the limits of my knowledge, especially about why anyone really does anything."

With that I agreed. Sometimes I'm clueless as to what motivates me, and I'm even less qualified to deduct accurately why others do what they do.

Still, I thought that Collins had been burdened (or blessed) with a martyr complex—that he wanted to save Jones and the camp; that he wanted his life to stand for something, even if he had to sacrifice it.

On the day of the offered plea agreement, Judge Grosshans turned to Collins and warned him that his guilty plea could result in his being sentenced to ten years in the state penitentiary and that a ten-thousand-dollar fine could also be imposed.

Collins said he understood.

Judge Grosshans then advised Collins again of the many rights he would enjoy if he went to trial—that he had a right to counsel, that the state had to prove its case beyond a reasonable doubt, that he didn't have to testify, that he was presumed innocent, and that the burden of proof rested on the prosecution. He was told that the jury had to agree unanimously on any verdict against him. As I read the transcript of the proceedings, I felt that the judge was essentially telling Collins, "I don't think you're guilty, and I don't think the state can prove it."

I agreed. How could the state prove Collins guilty of anything relying on the testimony of the proven murderer and liar by the name of James Lee Jones Jr.?

"Do you understand everything that I've said to you?" the judge asked.

"Yes" was Collins's simple answer.

"Do you have any questions that you want to put to me?"

"No," Collins said.

The judge hadn't given up. He probed further: "Have your attorneys been able to answer to your satisfaction all the questions that you may have put to them?"

"Yes," Collins said.

Still the judge wasn't satisfied: "You realize your attorneys have spent a lot of time preparing for the trial that's scheduled to commence in about ten days or two weeks?"

"Yes," Collins replied.

The judge: "You realize they have subpoenaed literally dozens of witnesses to testify on your behalf. You understand that?"

"Yes," Collins replied.

Then, obviously in the hope that Collins would sleep on it, the judge told him that he could delay entering his plea for another forty-eight hours—"to give you time to settle down and cool off."

Collins said he understood.

The judge stated it again: "You don't have to proceed with sentencing today, do you understand that?"

"Yes."

In what appeared to be the judge's last hope, he turned to Collins's defense attorneys. "Do you believe your client fully and completely understands what he is about to do?"

"I do," Viken said.

"Do you believe this to be a knowing and intelligent waiver?" the judge asked.

Viken said, "I believe that Collins Catch the Bear has come to a knowing and intelligent waiver and understanding of his rights in this matter, and that he can make an informed, intelligent judgment about it today, Judge. I believe that, yes."

The judge asked the same of Jim Leach, and got the same answer.

The judge then asked if any promises had been made to Collins, about the sentencing or disposition of his case.

Leach assured the judge that he knew of none.

The judge then invited Leach and Viken to further discuss the matter with their client. Leach said that would not be necessary.

Finally, the judge turned to Collins and said, "It is alleged that you committed the public offense of manslaughter in the second degree by recklessly killing Clarence Tollefson. To that allegation, what say you, guilty or not guilty?"

Collins replied, "Guilty." The record does not, of course, reveal the sound or timbre of his voice. Only the naked word admitting that he was a killer is recorded for history.

Still the judge wanted more. "Is this a plea of your own free will?"

Collins: "Yes."

Judge Grosshans: "Have you had enough time to think about this?"

Collins: "Yes."

Judge Grosshans: "Have you thought it over?"

Collins: "Yes."

The judge then read into the record that he found that Collins's plea "had been knowingly and freely and voluntarily entered with no promises having been made."

So, good-bye, Collins, for a long time, right?

No. Not yet. The judge now needed to hear from Collins's confession from his own lips. He turned to Collins and said, "Mr. Catch the Bear, now, in your own words, tell me what happened."

Collins began with the story we'd heard before. He and others—he didn't identify the others—were gathering wood for the camp. He said they took along a .22, in case they saw a deer or a turkey. He didn't say who owned the gun. Then he talked about coming upon Tollefson. Collins said that he was "wearing a knife around his chest," and as he jogged over to Tollefson, his knife was "flopping," and Tollefson said, "Don't try it." He thought the man's eyes were "funny," and Collins went back to the truck and said, "Let's go. This guy is crazy," but the others on the truck wanted to talk to him.

Collins then said that Tollefson got back in his camper and down out of sight. While the rest went over to talk to him, Collins stayed in the old green camp pickup. "I was scared of what he might do," Collins said. Then he said he heard "the mention that he had guns." It was then that Collins crawled through the open back window of the old truck and picked up the .22. At that point, other people whom he didn't identify were coming up to the ridge from the camp below.

Collins then said that he walked over to the passenger side of Tollefson's camper. He said one of his friends (unidentified) told him to put the gun away, "but I didn't listen to him because I was afraid." He said the window on the passenger side of Tollefson's camper was "open a foot and a half."

He then recounted how the argument between Tollefson and the Indians became loud and angry. Collins said he got into the argument as well, telling Tollefson, "You should get off this land, you white motherfucker. I lost my temper, but I wasn't thinking of killing him."

No intent.

"Then the chief of security, Jim Lee Jones, started to get aggressive with Mr. Tollefson, opened his door, tried to take his car keys, and Mr. Tollefson tried to pull the door closed, but Jim Jones was there blocking it, and then about that time, Jim Jones, he hit Mr. Tollefson in the chin, and started to pull him out of the pickup, and when I was on the passenger side, I seen the guns that Mr. Tollefson had.

"He had a pistol in his holster, pistol by his right thigh, maybe a foot away from his right thigh, and he had a rifle on the dashboard, and when Jim Lee Jones started to pull Mr. Tollefson out of his pickup, Mr. Tollefson reached for his pistol.

"First time he missed, second time he got hold of his pistol and he was bringing it up close by—almost right above the steering wheel, and I was thinking I got to do something, because he's going to kill somebody. And so I pulled up the .22 rifle that I had by my side, I put it in the window, and I pulled the trigger."

Killing in the defense of another: *a complete defense.*

From what I read in the record, Collins's intent was not to murder Tollefson, but to save James Lee Jones. He could be guilty of a homicide only if his conduct had been reckless.

But Judge Grosshans was finally ready to shore up his record. "You pulled the trigger of the gun that fatally killed Mr. Clarence Tollefson on July 21, 1982, in Pennington County, South Dakota?"

"Yes," Collins replied.

Judge Grosshans: "I am going to find there's a factual basis underlying your plea and, again, that it was knowingly, freely and voluntarily entered. I am going to accept your plea." The judge was ready to pronounce his sentence, but before he did, he asked Collins, "Do you, Mr. Catch the Bear, have anything that you want to say to me before I pronounce judgment in your case?"

Suddenly, Collins came alive. He said, "I'd like to tell you that the reason I was at the Yellow Thunder Camp is that all of my life I have been with people other than my own people. I don't talk my people's language, and by going out to the camp it was my chance to know the Indian way, and I went out there feeling that I'll get back to my people. So that's why I was out there. There is nothing about the camp that is radical to me. It is a beautiful place. It's for the children. I went out there not wanting to cause any problem with those people or to anybody else.

"I was trying to learn. I lived there for a while and I liked it there, and I think if I was put in the same position again, and somebody was threatening those people out there, the same thing would happen if I was in the same position. I know I sound like I'm cold-hearted, but I'm not. I feel for that man that got killed." (He didn't say "the man *I* killed.") "It would have been better if he could still be alive. I been having some feelings about him. I never knew him. I know I caused a lot of grief to people. I'm sorry for that, but it can't be changed. Things happen the way they happen and I'm sorry it happened that way, but that's just the way it happened."

Judge Grosshans: "Is that it?"

Collins: "Uh-huh," which was heard as a "yes."

Jeff Viken argued that two nonviolent men, Collins and Tollefson, had been met by a series of events set off by Jones, events that nobody could reverse once the violence turned to the use of firearms. He said that in South Dakota, two cultures had again collided, "two overlapping cultures that share this land, and there's no room for violence or firearms or anger, and out of which nothing comes until we look inside ourselves and try to understand that we've got to get on with living together, and until then there is not going to be any justice, not here."

Viken was right. Judge Grosshans's sentence, whatever it might be, could not render justice to the parties. He could only respond to the case presented. Even if this were a factually true case, he could only choose a judicial potion from his judicial medicine chest, one that would cure nothing nor prevent the spreading of the disease.

In passing, Viken spoke of Collins's "need to defend, the only thing Collins Catch the Bear understands," and he asked the judge for compassion.

Jim Leach told the judge, "Collins is a person I have cared very deeply about for a very long time." He thought that Collins "will make a positive future for himself and a way for himself in the world." Leach saw the brighter side: "It is a day of reckoning for him—it's a day of truth telling, and it's a day when he begins to face the rest of his life . . . Collins Catch the Bear went to Yellow Thunder Camp for the purpose of trying to find himself, his people, his language, his culture and his religion. I believe that his plea today does justice. I believe that it allows him to fully face his moral responsibility for his part in the death of Clarence Tollefson and allows him one day to seek again, in the free world, his culture and his people." He wanted the judge to find the positive in Collins that "all of us have been privileged to know."

The judge then turned to the state's attorney, Dennis Groff.

Groff said he thought the Tollefson family had been deceived into thinking that the prosecutors had "some sort of a guaranteed case here. The Tollefson family didn't know that our case rested upon the testimony of a convicted killer . . ."

Groff said the Tollefson family "wanted one thing—the truth, and they didn't get it, so my predecessor [Lefholz] decided we would buy the truth from James Jones[,] and it came at a heavy price. I want to leave it at that." Groff then conceded that Jeff Viken was right, "that it just wasn't the .22 on the other side of the four-wheel-drive that led to this man's death, that it was our key witness we've heard so much about [Jones] that initiated this conflict and created that moment where a shot was fired. I don't have anything good to say about James Jones either."

I believed that Groff had his own doubts about who had actually shot Clarence Tollefson.

Then Groff confessed what I had argued all along. He said, "I believe there was more than a probability, it was almost certain that if he [Collins had gone] to Sioux Falls [for the scheduled jury trial,] he would have been acquitted."

Groff said he didn't "buy that somehow this was a self-defense issue." He said Tollefson was scared that day, surrounded by as many as twelve people, and his instincts cost him his life when the state's key witness (Jones) began to pull him out of the vehicle. Groff said he thought that none of what Tollefson had said justified what happened to him. He ended by saying, "I am sorry we have had this day. I am sorry for every error I have seen on the record in the last three years. This may be the only way we could save this case and learn the truth. I am not proud to be here. I am proud to be with this family (the Tollefsons). I am proud to know we are going to have a solution to this case which maybe none of us want, but at least the cover-up is finally stopped."

Was it?

Groff asked for the maximum sentence.

The judge turned to Mrs. Tollefson and asked if she wanted to address the court. She said in a quiet voice, "My husband was a man who loved the Hills just as Catch the Bear loved the Hills." She thought her husband had been there that day "because he was looking to see what condition the camp was in. We moved into our home here, and he said, 'This is where I want to live and die,' and ironically, he died maybe only two miles from where I live. His rights were violated that day and that's what I carry in my heart and want that acknowledged."

The judge was ready to sum up before he sentenced Collins Catch the Bear. He said he agreed with Groff, the new prosecutor, that the case Groff had taken over was one that "had been tampered with." The judge also agreed with Groff that his prosecution could not be based on the testimony of James Lee Jones. "One thing that has always bothered me," the judge confessed, "is the unholy alliance the state and federal government made with Mr. James Lee Jones."

The judge, a man, then pronounced his sentence on a mere boy (but a man in the blind eyes of the law): ten years, the maximum allowed by the law. I thought the judge's sentence hurt him, words delivered dry-eyed though the tears of his soul.

But the judge included ways to mitigate the sentence. He gave Collins credit for the time he'd been incarcerated awaiting the final disposition of his case—from September 17, 1982, to February 19, 1985, and his eligibility for parole would be computed from the earlier date. Also, the sentence would run concurrently with the five-year sentence imposed for his escape from the halfway house in Rapid City. "Concurrent" meant he'd serve both sentences at the same time. It looked to me like Collins could be up for parole in a year or two, and everyone might live happily ever after.

24.

Time. Relentless, mindless Time. It chews away at itself and is never satisfied. By the summer of 1986, Paul Ruder, Pactola District ranger for the U.S. Forest Service, had made his report on the Yellow Thunder Camp: "There haven't been more than five people there all summer long. Last winter was the first time no one was up there."

Today, no visible signs of the camp remain. The rushing, happy sounds of the early spring runoff can be heard at the creek. Here and there, the land is blotted with scattered garbage left by tourists.

Following my last encounter with Collins Catch the Bear, three decades sped carelessly by. During those years, Collins had been paroled, released, reconvicted of nonviolent crimes associated with his alcoholism, and paroled and released again to face the bitter outside world. He was like a small, featherless bird dropped in the middle of South Dakota in January. The longing for *place* had given way to the simple, cruel will to survive.

On May 19, 1997, about ten years before Collins's death, Jim Leach, who had just completed a visit with him in Rapid City, wrote me, "Collins looks real different. I wouldn't have recognized him if I hadn't been expecting to see him. He looks old. He looks older than I look. He looked to me like he is in his 50s. He is slightly balding in the front."

On that same day, Collins wrote me. His lengthy, apologetic letter stated in part:

> I am writing this letter to thank both you and Mr. Moriarity for the gracious help which you both gave to me in 1982–1983. I know that without your help I would likely still be in jail.

On May 29, 1997, I replied:

> Collins,
>   Thanks for your letter. Your thanks was a gift back to me. You are a whole, beautiful person. Believe it. Judge yourself with love. It is hard to find your way as a white man finds his. Perhaps there are other ways that will open to you.
>   Be open—
>   Waiting—
>   Loving.
>   Gerry Spence

Collins's reprieves from jails and prisons often left him living on the street. He once wrote Jim that he'd been offered a job as a dishwasher. Whether he showed up for work is not recorded.

Then came this note from Jim to me on May 20, 1999:

> Collins was in prison for unlawful entry to a motor vehicle. He was mixing vodka and cough medicine, and fought with a police officer. Says he loves me. I tell him I love him. Says he was diagnosed with paranoid schizophrenia . . . Says he's been locked up for 13 of the 17 years

since he was 19 . . . but I never would have known it from spending the day with him. He is polite and direct and does not act "institutionalized" or angry.

He asked me to drive him out to the old Yellow Thunder Camp. We went out there and walked around. We talked about those days.

Nothing in Jim's letter suggested that they talked about Collins's guilty plea in the Tollefson case.

Later, Jim sent me a letter from Collins dated July 16, 1999. He wrote that he had been transferred to the state prison in Jamestown, North Dakota:

> I'm back in prison because I started drinking, and I know that if I am to stay free I must completely abstain from alcohol. If I stay out of trouble in here I am looking at about thirteen months.

By August 31, 2000, Collins wrote Jim that he just gotten out of jail in Bismarck and would be starting a minimum-wage job the next day. But by May 4, 2001, he had called Jim to tell him that he had received a five-year sentence with five years' probation for assault on a police officer, and that he'd been in custody since December 2000 for that offense. He told Jim, "I let the bottle get the best of me again. This is the seventh time I've been in the North Dakota State Prison."

On December 3, 2004, Collins had been in custody in Wakpala, in north-central South Dakota. Released in April of that year, he traveled down to Rapid City to visit Jim, where he got drunk. He was incarcerated in the Pennington County Jail in Rapid City as an "absconder," apparently for having violated his parole by leaving the Wakpala area without permission.

By April 26, 2005, Collins was in jail in Bismarck, North Dakota. Jim notes that he sent Collins a book he'd wanted. Collins then wrote Jim that he had been sentenced to thirty months for some unidentified crime and that he should be out in about two years.

On July 18, 2005, Collins wrote Jim from prison in North Dakota, thanking him for his birthday gift, a fifty-dollar money order, and asking if he could arrange for him a subscription to the *Jerusalem Post*, a leading Jewish newspaper. Jim did so.

On September 19, 2007, Collins called Jim from Bismarck to report that his sister Sharon had died two weeks before. As for Collins, he was living on the street. Jim reported that Collins told him, "I love you, bro," and Jim replied, "I love you, too, Collins."

Jim told me, "On December 6, 2007, I sent Collins money for a bus ticket to San Diego. I did not want him to freeze to death in winter in North Dakota. On January 3, 2008, Collins called me from North Dakota, saying he did not get on the bus to San Diego. He said he thinks the ticket is still good and he may still go there. He said he was calling to "get straight with me." This was the last time Jim heard from Collins Catch the Bear.

In some ways, Jim Leach took care of Collins as if he were a wayward son. I think most men have a set of father-son genes lurking around in them. I asked Jim if his loyal, seemingly irreversible caring for Collins didn't have something to do with that. He said he hadn't really considered it, but he thought not.

On the twenty-seventh day of January 2008, at eight minutes past one in the afternoon, Collins Spencer Catch the Bear was trying to cross eight lanes of highway, four lanes each way, on Interstate 8 a few miles east of San Diego. An oncoming motorist was unable to avoid hitting him. The authorities could not determine why he attempted to cross the freeway. Upon arrival, medics tried CPR but were unsuccessful.

The chief medical examiner reported that Collins's blood alcohol level was .28 percent, which is beyond the point at which most men black out. The legal limit is .08 percent for adults in California. His blood also contained evidence of recent use of marijuana. The report recited: "He had a tattoo of CCTB noted on his left forearm and a large partially healed cut to his right forearm. Numerous cut mark scars were noted to both wrists[,] possibly indicative of previous suicide attempts." At last, Collins was safe and provided with a sanitary resting place. "He was secured in a new white vinyl pouch and a blue tamper-proof seal was affixed." The examiner's record reported that no next of kin was found. His remains were buried at Saint Elizabeth Cemetery, Wakpala, South Dakota.

Russell Means died on October 22, 2012, a month short of his seventy-third birthday. He was an activist, a writer, an actor, an agitator, a renegade, a brash showman, and a hero. He was crafty, cunning, outspoken, and, yes, courageous. Those remaining safely hidden from the fray have criticized his antics and his causes. Still, Means devoted his life in a sometimes single-handed fight for the rights of Indian people. His ashes were spread over the Black Hills, including Yellow Thunder Camp.

Bruce Ellison, a widely known and respected criminal defense lawyer, defended many Indians, including Russell Means. Ellison never compromised his principles or his voice in his fight for Indian people. He continues his good work in the law.

Jim Leach is a respected, successful practicing trial lawyer in Rapid City and has earned the highest ratings offered by the organizations that evaluate trial lawyers. He has been a member of our staff at my Trial Lawyers College and represents only people, not corporations or insurance companies. His lifetime of pro bono work for the America Indian has repeatedly proven his commitment to their cause. I am proud to include him as one of my personal friends.

My former partner Eddie Moriarity is still practicing law. He is one of the great human beings on the face of this earth. I love him like my son and admire him as a peer. His commitment to justice and to his clients is exemplary. He works out of an honest and loving heart, something rarely observed or appreciated in lawyers for the people. He has offices in Missoula, Montana.

Judge Roland E. Grosshans died on June 7, 2012, of Lou Gehrig's disease, having retired after a distinguished career as state's attorney for ten years and as a South Dakota jurist for sixteen years. His attempt to save Collins Catch the Bear is among his most admirable work from the bench. It restores our hope for judges who are willing to serve justice even at their own expense.

Rodney Lefholz, sixty-seven, is engaged in a selective, out-of-court practice in Rapid City. He remained out of politics after he was defeated in his early bid for attorney general and for reelection as state's attorney. He and his wife have three grown children and four grandchildren.

I talked with Mr. Lefholz these thirty years later and found him to be open and candid. When I asked him about using No Heart Jones as his chief witness, he said, "As a prosecutor, you do the best you can with the witnesses you've got."

Lefholz thought that Collins's best defense was that the killing of Tollefson was committed in the defense of another. "It was a pretty solid defense," Lefholz said. "But his lawyers might have thought that a good defense won't always get you an acquittal." I agreed.

My darling Imaging is as alive, perceptive, insightful, and beautiful as she was the first day I saw her. I have wondered if she wasn't born under a magic tree in the forest. She has been a loving guide though the forest of my life, not to mention through the mothering of my four children and her two along with our thirteen grandchildren. She is a friend to many; an artist, a designer, a philosopher, a teacher, a coach, a businesswoman—in short, a miracle. No man has ever been so blessed or so loved.

I am in my ninetieth year and still riding one of the wooden horses that swings up and down on life's merry-go-round, keeping time to the carnival music of being.

Epilogue

I've found myself asking, "What is this story about? And why did I feel compelled to tell it after all these many years?" It is, of course, a partial and imperfect record of the tragic life of Collins Catch the Bear. But the question remains: does such a life stand for anything?

In the lives of the few who are chosen, a moment arrives when they are called upon to acknowledge their gift, and to respond. Across the annals of time, heroes from humble origins have provided us with examples of self-sacrifice and courage that have changed the course of history. That moment came for Collins Catch the Bear when he was betrayed by James Lee "Wambli No Heart" Jones.

Someone had to answer for the Indians' killing of the white man Clarence Tollefson. How would white power have responded if Collins had been acquitted? Would it have fomented another white-Indian war like Wounded Knee? Would white power have risen up in unleashed outrage and smashed the last flutter of life from Yellow Thunder Camp?

Perhaps Collins believed his plea would save the camp. Or perhaps he'd simply grown weary of the struggle. Or, as Rodney Lefholz observed, Collins might have been advised that although he had a good defense, a good defense does not guarantee an acquittal. Some argued that Collins, in fact, killed Clarence Tollefson and then pled guilty because he was overcome by guilt. Others suggest that prison life was the only life he knew, providing him with food, shelter, and reasonable safety.

In the end, I found myself looking for an argument to satisfy my own need: to write the life's story of a modern-day Indian hero. I was looking for an argument to support my conclusion that Collins was a hero. I found the facts wanting. I felt that I had wasted my life by joining Collins and writing about his wasted life. So, why should I ask unsuspecting readers to join us as well?

I knew that Collins loved the Yellow Thunder Camp, and I believe he agreed to take the blame for Tollefson's death to save the camp. I began to see him as a modern-day martyr, for as history habitually confirms, martyrs are human, and as such, they possess their own collection of sins and weaknesses.

I began to think of a few of history's best-known martyrs. Socrates comes to mind. He was one of the world's great philosophers and most famous martyrs. He was offered the chance to escape but, remaining true to his teachings, refused, and died peacefully drinking the hemlock.

In the Christian world, Christ is our most famous martyr. And nearly all his disciples suffered martyrdom—beheading, crucifixion; Peter was crucified upside down—all dying for the sake of Christ's teachings.

I remembered Joan of Arc, the peasant girl who became the savior of France and was burned at the stake for heresy.

And I thought of Nathan Hale, who famously lamented, "I regret that I have but one life to lose for my country."

I was willing to leave this book by positing this question to the reader: Was Collins Catch the Bear a martyr for his people, or was his life the chronicle of a hopeless drunk?

I put these pages away to let time help answer that question.

Then, one night not long ago, I awoke stunned with a realization that had been hiding in the foggy backcountry of my mind. I had ended the book at the point at which *I* wanted to stop, not where the story ended. What had happened to James Lee Jones? I'd all but forgotten him. Frankly, I hadn't much cared. Nevertheless, on January 23, 2015, I wrote Jim Leach a dutiful email inquiring.

Jim wrote back:

> Here is what floored me. I assume you remember—maybe a poor assumption—that after Jones testified against Collins, Lefholz wrote to the U.S. Parole Commission saying that Jones had reformed and now was a good bet to become a law-abiding citizen, and Jones was paroled in late 1983. Two years later, on February 17, 1986, Jones committed another murder, this one in Tennessee.
>
> He was sentenced to death.

Jim retrieved for me the published court decisions regarding Jones's case. In one decision, the judge recited some of the salient facts surrounding the robbery and murder committed by Jones. The judge wrote that Jones's victim "was bound, gagged, and blindfolded with duct tape. The victim was distressed and crying and begging not to be hurt. Jones stood over him and stabbed him six times, four times penetrating the heart. He then watched as the victim went into convulsions, blood spewing from the nose and mouth."

Jones's accomplice testified against him, thereby saving his own life, a betrayal with which Jones was well acquainted. The accomplice testified that Jones "was working himself up on a rhythm";

he was "cool" and "under control." Jones was awarded the death penalty, and that catapulted him into years of habeas corpus hearings and years more of appeals through various courts in an effort to save his life.

By 1998, Jones had taken on yet another identity: Abu-Ali Abdur'Rahman, a Muslim holy man. Predictably, the change of name and profession did not change the man. The published court decisions burden us with the tragic personal history of Jones, the nature of which one might have suspected.

As a child, Jones became the victim of unspeakably vile and degenerate abuse. One of the judges recounts that Jones's mother put him, his infant half sister, and two brothers in a taxi and then rode with them to the woods and left them there. The taxi driver went back, retrieved the children, and turned them over to the state.

The same judge recounted how Jones received regular beatings with a leather strap from his father, who also "made him take off his clothes, placed him hog-tied in a locked closet, and tethered him to a hook with a piece of leather tied around the head of his penis. Then his father struck Jones' penis with a baseball bat. To punish him for smoking, his father required him to eat a pack of cigarettes, and when he vomited, was made to eat the vomit."

The judge wrote, "None of this extraordinary abuse, which constitutes relevant mitigating evidence, was heard by the jury. This was a grave omission by defense counsel." One wonders who the killer actually was: Jones's father, who'd laid cruel, degenerate hands on a helpless child, or that child himself, who years later, as an adult, took the murder weapon into his own hands?

One might wonder why Jones's history of these childhood horrors hadn't been offered to the jury to reduce his penalty from death to life in prison. An abundance of other mitigating evidence was also available to Jones's attorneys. His wife "spoke effervescently about her husband. 'Well, when I first met James and he opened up his mouth, it was like thunder from heaven . . . I was fascinated with James . . . he was different, just different from any man I had ever met. He wanted to do something for the world. I was intrigued by that.'"

A former fiancée, now an attorney, testified that "when she knew the Petitioner (Jones) in 1983, he held a steady job, attended college, and performed volunteer work with a Quaker youth group at Cabrini Green, a large, infamous public housing development in Chicago known for its poverty and violence." She described Jones as gentle, caring, and filled with dignity, a person with whom she shared a sincere Christian belief. The jury heard nothing of this sort from any witness, and according to one judge, the defendant's counsel was "substantially ineffective and Jones was thereby deprived of a constitutionally fair trial."

Still, the U.S. Court of Appeals for the Sixth Circuit affirmed his death sentence, and the U.S. Supreme Court denied certiorari—the High Court's way of saying, "We will not even look at your case beyond refusing to look at it."

But Judge R. Guy Cole Jr. of the Sixth Circuit, in a dissent couched in splendid language, exposed the empty logic and rhetoric of the majority: "Deploying the familiar logic of the double-edged sword, the majority obliterated in a few sentences the mitigating value of Abdur'Rahman's horrific upbringing—the worst case of abuse the testifying psychologist had seen in twenty-five years of practice." Indeed, Judge Cole believed that had a jury heard this evidence, at least one juror would have refused to impose the death penalty. And that would have saved Abdur'Rahman's life.

Beyond that, the dissenting judge laid out a case against the prosecutor that included willful withholding of evidence that tended to mitigate justification for the death penalty. Though he knew that Abdur'Rahman (Jones) had been mentally disturbed, "the prosecutor *lied* to defense counsel, telling him that no evidence mitigated Abdur'Rahman's prior crime," and with pernicious invention, the prosecutor claimed that the killing was committed in furtherance of a drug turf war. The dissenting judge wrote, "The drug-turf-war fabrication devastated the defense, and the fallout entailed much more than the missed opportunity to present the suppressed evidence." In short, the judge argued that Abdur'Rahman faced death rather than life imprisonment not because of his crime but because the prosecutor had lied him into the death house. The judge's conclusion is worth repeating in whole:

> A parting thought. Whatever your take on the merits of Abdur'Rahman claims, one thing about this case is undeniable: the prosecutor desecrated his noble role. He failed grossly in his duty to act as "the representative of a sovereignty whose interest in a criminal prosecution is not that it shall win a case, but that justice shall be done." Abdur'Rahman may face the ultimate penalty as a result; Justice will bear the scar.

Jim Leach ended his email of January 23, 2015, to me with, "Anyway I just googled Jones. Apparently his execution is now scheduled for October 6, 2015." Jones has since been granted a reprieve. At this writing, he remains on death row, but he is breathing and, without doubt, suffering the torture the law inflicts on those who suffer the interminable wait to be murdered by a justice system that murders those who murder.

I am now compelled to write a new conclusion. And I will. Many of the Indians who once occupied the camp are dead or gone or are rotting in the white man's prisons. Yet, the Lakota have survived the white man's shameful chronicle of broken promises and treaties and white power's efforts to exterminate Indian culture. Many of the Indian people, steeped in the richness of their brave and bloody history, strive to make a difference by carrying on the traditions of the tribe. And in the face of overwhelming challenges, many Lakota live responsible and productive lives, and fight on.

The camp has been taken up and digested by the insatiable appetite of Mother Nature. Only scattered remnants can be seen: the ubiquitous broken beer bottle and, here and there, a piece of discarded junk protruding from forgiving spring grasses. The tepees are gone, but sometimes the sounds of children remain— no longer the happy cacophony of Indian children, but the laughter and excitement of visiting white children innocently playing along the clear, rushing stream.

The dream of a return to the Indian way has been lost with Time's transportation of the Sioux into the hostile present. Many have been absorbed into the dominant white culture and struggle to escape the deadly disease of poverty and the evils endemic in the white man's world.

The tragic life of Collins Catch the Bear reminds us of the potential courage of man, of his will to live even through the ravages of pain and disgrace, and that the power of love is abiding. Collins's martyrdom stands as an escaping beam of hesitant hope in a cruel and fearsome world.

We cannot read these pages without a sense of despair. I feel it as I write. The diseases of hate and prejudice are grossly contagious. Like bacteria in a petri dish, hate multiplies, contaminating all that it touches. Blameless children, Collins Catch the Bear and James Lee Jones Jr., were neglected, abused, and tortured by parents whose lives would have tarnished the reputation of sewer rats. Who we have become, for good or otherwise, has much to do not only with the seed that is planted, but also with the gardeners who tend the crop.

At last a sense of joy seeps up though these hard, dark pages. It is an approaching awareness that Collins got his wish. He became a blessed martyr for his people. I can see his high cheekbones, his long hair, a pair of plain, black-rimmed glasses, his face as innocent and solemn as a saint's. This small, slight man, unburdened with body strength but possessing a soul's capacity to endure endless degradation, pain, and relentless loss, heroically played to the end the game of life to which he had been assigned. Death always provides past lives with new meaning. Had I stared at Collins Catch the Bear long enough, I was convinced, a timid halo might have appeared.

And now?

How could the story of his life provide a message for his people and for us? I cannot understand the meaning of the life of Collins Catch the Bear without recognizing that his beauty and his blemishes, and his struggle with both, provide hope and instruction for those who have been confronted with lesser challenges and with more of life's gifts to overcome them.

Is it not my duty to find the sun in this shadowed world? I think not. I shall leave the search to you, for the effort at discovery will always prove to be its own reward.